CAMBRIDGE LIBRARY COLLECTION

Books of enduring scholarly value

Linguistics

From the earliest surviving glossaries and translations to nineteenth-century academic philology and the growth of linguistics during the twentieth century, language has been the subject both of scholarly investigation and of practical handbooks produced for the upwardly mobile, as well as for travellers, traders, soldiers, missionaries and explorers. This collection will reissue a wide range of texts pertaining to language, including the work of Latin grammarians, groundbreaking early publications in Indo-European studies, accounts of indigenous languages, many of them now extinct, and texts by pioneering figures such as Jacob Grimm, Wilhelm von Humboldt and Ferdinand de Saussure.

Hausa Grammar

Charles Henry Robinson (1861–1925) was a Cambridge scholar who, during the 1890s, published several books on the language, literature and culture of the Hausa people. Hausa is an African language originating in Niger and northern Nigeria and spoken widely in West and Central Africa as a lingua franca. Published in 1897, Robinson's *Grammar* was written to serve the needs of missionaries, colonial staff and army officers who wished to communicate with the local people, but made no claim to be definitive or comprehensive. Until the twentieth century Hausa was written in an Arabic script, examples of which are given, while the exercise sections of the grammar are transliterated for students unfamiliar with Arabic. The vocabulary, mainly relating to agriculture, trade and domestic life, was chosen to suit the practical needs of Robinson's intended audience, and reveals much about colonial life in West Africa as well as providing linguistic information.

Cambridge University Press has long been a pioneer in the reissuing of out-of-print titles from its own backlist, producing digital reprints of books that are still sought after by scholars and students but could not be reprinted economically using traditional technology. The Cambridge Library Collection extends this activity to a wider range of books which are still of importance to researchers and professionals, either for the source material they contain, or as landmarks in the history of their academic discipline.

Drawing from the world-renowned collections in the Cambridge University Library, and guided by the advice of experts in each subject area, Cambridge University Press is using state-of-the-art scanning machines in its own Printing House to capture the content of each book selected for inclusion. The files are processed to give a consistently clear, crisp image, and the books finished to the high quality standard for which the Press is recognised around the world. The latest print-on-demand technology ensures that the books will remain available indefinitely, and that orders for single or multiple copies can quickly be supplied.

The Cambridge Library Collection will bring back to life books of enduring scholarly value (including out-of-copyright works originally issued by other publishers) across a wide range of disciplines in the humanities and social sciences and in science and technology.

Hausa Grammar

With Exercises, Readings and Vocabulary

Charles Henry Robinson

CAMBRIDGE
UNIVERSITY PRESS

CAMBRIDGE UNIVERSITY PRESS

Cambridge, New York, Melbourne, Madrid, Cape Town,
Singapore, São Paolo, Delhi, Tokyo, Mexico City

Published in the United States of America by Cambridge University Press, New York

www.cambridge.org
Information on this title: www.cambridge.org/9781108031370

This edition first published 1897
This digitally printed version 2011

ISBN 978-1-108-03137-0 Paperback

HAUSA GRAMMAR.

بسم الله الرحمن الرحيم صلى الله على سيدنا محمد وآله وصحبه وسلم

هذا الكتاب الدراعة لمنسوب

سورة التوبة الله فاروا انفروا اثر	بسم الله الله فاروا انفروا اذكر فبارزايك
يا الله رب لحمام عمعا اخترنا	فما ذكرى مثل الله عافتنا ملاني
يا الله يا خالق يا ازووس سرونا	يا معبود يا رب تبا اسرك سرونا
يا الله كشترير موازكهوان	كذا منكركم هيم اية نبيش حماب
دامرفاته بن الرحمن كلام	باونا ذكيم بث يا بشكنكربا
نعماتم الماجر الخمير هذا	كنا ذكر خنا الله ما اكرا ملاني
اكونيتا اكترتردكا ووازكنا	كترتردكا اكتر ما استداد انف
حتم كروا ذكرتكم ذم دعواالله	رائنا فمر خترنك بتر بسعدى
انا نقيلانا انكم انا فسادا	وتر انا اكر داقسا يكمربا ايش
اسووبا دقوفانوفي اترنكم	ابركنكم ابتر نا عيا دا بمة بعد
اسووبا نعاالله ابر نقر مخورا	نشكر نعوبا كذا انا اكبر سكمربا
بلزنقب سر ستدنا سعد سترك	مروبا دنم فزونيلاسر كوفيا
اكرورزوبم له بر برا باس دبروا	وكاد وبا نا كونوذكابا كريس
ذاسرا اسادكا دلنشز روا عداسا	نكم ميس نكر ماتلانكم مصنا
كم نعر بغير كركم ربا عمر عذابا	ستا كوكا سنا سنا اسشكر نكي
سم هتر نكابيم بيا ونا ددنتا	نثنا نقر اسا اشكركم السكارا
كهبه هنبد بيت كمرس با كلاقا	مينوبا بسم كم كاتم بمر نقابر
انعيا نعاالله ابوك اتر نكرما	ايكوايا بنس نهرد داشي مخذرعذابا
نوايذ امنا	اتركج اعمووآند
مرملابلاكرب كى نعزبار دنسارا	بارتهس يا كوراكرسانكرعنابا
كنا ادم ما انخا ركاد حتى	كتم الله كبر سونع سرنسم نبس

كبرمكر

HAUSA GRAMMAR

WITH

EXERCISES, READINGS AND VOCABULARY

BY THE REV.

CHARLES H. ROBINSON M.A.

Lecturer in Hausa in the University of Cambridge
author of 'Hausaland or Fifteen Hundred Miles through the Central Soudan',
'Specimens of Hausa Literature' etc.

LONDON
KEGAN PAUL, TRENCH, TRÜBNER & Co., Ltd.
PATERNOSTER HOUSE, CHARING CROSS ROAD.
1897.

PRINTED BY E. J. BRILL, LEIDEN (HOLLAND).

CONTENTS.

	Page.
Introduction .	1.
Pronouns .	15.
The Verb	24.
Substantives. The plural	29.
" Gender .	34.
Numerals .	38.
Adjectives	42.
Adverbs .	47.
Prepositions .	49.
Conjunctions.	51.
Interjections .	53.
Additional Grammatical Notes .	55.
Common or Idiomatic Expression	62.

HAUSA READINGS.

Introductory Note .	67.
I. Extract from Hausa Poem, with facsimile .	69.
II. The Lord's Prayer with notes, etc.	72.
III. Story of capture of Khartum.	75.
IV. The Pilgrimmage to Mecca .	79.
V. Letter to the king of Zinder	83.
VI. The country of the ravens	86.

VOCABULARY.

Hausa—English	92.
English—Hausa	106.
Note	122.

ABBREVIATIONS.

A. B. C. etc. followed by numerals refer to poems published in 'Specimens of Hausa Literature'.
A. or Ar. Arabic.
f. feminine.
L. followed by a numeral. Lesson.
m. masculine.
pl. plural.

CORRIGENDA AND ADDENDA

page 5 line 6 add after 'Augustine', de Civ. Dei XVI. 6.
„ 17 „ 23 for 'possesseor' read 'possessor'.
„ 21 „ 15 „ makoiyo „ makoiya.
„ 22 „ 2 „ 'interrogaiive' „ 'interrogative'.
„ 22 „ 6 add 'wonni, f. wache, which, what? (agreeing with noun)'.
„ 26 „ 8 for 'on' read 'or'
„ 27 „ 3 (from bottom) for ga read ya.
„ 31 „ 6 add after 'furayi', 'or furare'.
„ 31 „ 17 for kawosu' read kawosu?
„ 46 „ 23 for maretchi read marechi.
„ 47 „ 4 (from bottom) maretchi read marechi.
„ 47 „ 17 for 'of nearly' read 'or nearly'.
„ 60 column 1. after 'shina' add 'or yana'.

„ 83 line 18 for كَثِر read كَثِى.
„ 84 „ 15 after masufeshe add ba.
„ 84 „ 16 „ sariki omit ba.
„ 84 „ 18 for wotiki read wotika.

„ 86 „ 11 „ سُرِكِ read سَرِكِ.

„ 86 „ 14 „ غَرِنْكُ „ عَرِنْكُ.

„ 87 „ 11 before يَشِغَ read بَا.

„ 88 „ 19 for china read chira.
„ 90 „ 9 init. add 'folded (it) up in'.
„ 105 „ 6 (column 2) for 'comen' read 'come'.

PREFACE.

The present work does not pretend to be in any sense a full or complete grammar of the Hausa language. So little attention has hitherto been paid to the study of this language, and so few Europeans have ever penetrated into the Hausa country, that adequate materials for the compilation of a complete grammar are not as yet available. The author would have preferred to wait for some considerable time further, had it not been the case that a short practical introduction to the study of the language was in immediate request for the use both of missionaries, and of officers in command of the Hausa troops in English employ, on the west coast of Africa.

Inasmuch as the fifteen millions of Hausa-speaking people in the Western and Central Soudan are now included within the sphere of British influence the importance of the Hausa language is likely to be increasingly recognised in the near future.

Within the past year it has been added to the list of languages which candidates for the post of student-interpreter in the British Army are invited to present for examination.

For the sake of beginners who may be ignorant of the Arabic alphabet the first part of the grammar has been transliterated into the Roman character. As however it is impossible for anyone to make any considerable progress in the study of the language without being able to read it as it is written by the natives, I have added some specimens of Hausa composition in the ordinary Arabic type and a facsimile of their actual handwriting.

In compiling the present work I have obtained a large amount of help from the 'Grammar of the Hausa language' published in 1862 by Rev. J. F. SCHÖN, formerly a missionary of the Church Missionary Society.

Great credit is due to Dr. SCHÖN for the many years, which he spent in the study of this language both at Sierra Leone and afterwards in England. He took part in the government expedition which ascended the Niger in 1841 for the sake of exploring the course of the River, but was unfortunately never able to penetrate into the Hausa country, and, as he afterwards spoke of himself as having reduced to writing a' hitherto-unwritten language, was apparently unaware of the existence of any native writing or literature. He may, however, justly be regarded as the pioneer of Hausa study, and although I have found myself unable to agree with a large number of statements contained in his grammar, I desire to acknowledge the immense help which it proved to me, in commencing the study of the language. For a complete list of books hitherto published on the Hausa language I would refer to pp. XVIII and XIX of my 'Specimens of Hausa Literature' recently published by the Cambridge University Press.

I am indebted for the Specimen Reading N°. VI and for several of the notes appended to it to Mr. HERMANN HARRIS of Gabes, Tunis; also to Mr. A. H. TURNER, one of H. M. Consuls in West Africa, Mr. W. H. BROOKS of Christ's College Cambridge and Dr. T. J. TONKIN for considerable help in the correction of the proofs of this grammar and for several suggestions which I have been able to adopt. Dr. TONKIN was my companion in my recent journey through the Hausa States, and I am particularly indebted to him for many colloquial phrases relating to trade and travelling, his knowledge of which phrases, when we were together in the country, so often proved superior to my own. My special thanks are due to the Syndics of the Cambridge University Press for permission to insert the facsimile specimen of Hausa writing from 'Specimens of Hausa Literature'. I should like to express my gratitude also to the publishers of this grammar for the very great trouble to which they have been put in the course of its publication.

The student, who is acquainted with Arabic, will observe a considerable number of words in the grammar which are obviously borrowed from Arabic in addition to a still larger number which are probably to be connected with Arabic roots. I have not made any attempt to point out the connection between Hausa and Arabic, as this will naturally be attempted in a dictionary, on the compilation of which I am at present engaged.

The system of transliteration which I have adopted is that originally propounded by the Royal Geographical Society. It has been sanctioned by the British Go-

vernment and, with one or two unimportant modifications, by nearly all the Governments of Enrope for the
representation of the sound of geographical names. The
general principle of the system is this: all vowels are
pronounced as in Italian, all consonants as in English:
every letter is pronounced and no redundant letters are
introduced. The details of the system are more fully
explained on pp. 13, 14. In a very few instances I
have placed an accent over a vowel in order to indicate that the emphasis falls on a particular syllable.
As, however, this emphasis differs a good deal in different places, I have made but very sparing use of such
accents.

The student is advised to mark the list of errata in
the text of the book, also to read carefully the note
which follows the Vocabulary, before commencing to
study the grammar.

CHAS H. ROBINSON.

June 20. 1897.
Trinity College Cambridge.

INTRODUCTION.

Hausa is probably the most widely spoken language on the continent of Africa. The country inhabited by the Hausas, extending roughly speaking, from lat. 8 N. to 14 N., and from long. 4 E. to 11 E., and including about half a million square miles, contains a population which is estimated at twenty five millions. Of these no less than fifteen millions speak the Hausa language, or, in other words, the Hausa speaking people form one per cent of the whole population of the world. Hausa moreover acts as a sort of *lingua franca*, and as the language of trade, far outside the actual limits of Hausaland. Settlements of Hausa-speaking people are to be found in places as far separated from one another as Suakim, Alexandria, Tripoli, Tunis and Lagos; and Hausa caravans are constantly passing to and fro between all these places and Hausaland proper. It is by no means inconceivable that the day may yet come when four languages will dominate the entire continent of Africa. These will be English, Arabic, Swahili and Hausa. English will be the language of the south, Arabic of the north, whilst Swahili and Hausa will divide between them eastern and western tropical Africa.

Apart from the wide spread of the language in the

present and its prospects for the future, the study of Hausa should prove of interest owing to its possible connection in early times with the Semitic group of languages. A great deal of careful work will have to be done before it will be possible to prove or disprove such a connection or to suggest any definite theory in regard to the early history of the Hausa language. It is at present surrounded by some half a dozen other languages, no one of which has as yet been thoroughly mastered by any European student, and the study of which will no doubt throw considerable light upon the problem. In the few remarks which I should like to make here as to the possible connection between Hausa and the Semitic languages I may perhaps be allowed to quote a few sentences from the introduction to my recently published 'Specimens of Hausa Literature' pp. X—XII.

'At first sight it would certainly seem as though Hausa had very strong claims to be regarded as a definitely Semitic language. Quite a third of the words which it contains are obviously connected with Semitic roots. The names for many of the commonest things, with which the Hausas must have been familiar from the very earliest times, are apparently of Semitic origin.

Their pronouns, with two or perhaps three exceptions, are Semitic. The connection between Hausa and the Semitic languages — or, what here comes to the same thing, between Hausa and Arabic — is far closer than can be at all satisfactorily explained on the supposition that the former has simply been modified by the latter, as the result of the spread of Mohammedanism in the country, an event which has only occurred within the present century. As an additional reason for assuming the possibility of a Semitic origin for the language may be mentioned the fact that the general belief of the Hausa people is that in very early time their ancestors came from the far east away beyond Mecca. The difficulties on the other hand in the way of regarding it as a definitely Semitic language are very great, if not insuperable. Two-thirds of the vocabulary bears no resemblance whatever to Arabic, the harsh guttural sounds of the Arabic are altogether wanting, and the existence of triliteral roots, the distinctive characteristic of the Semitic languages, is, to say the least, extremely doubtful.

In attempts which have been made to classify the modern languages of Africa it has been the usual custom to place those as yet examined under one of three groups, viz. Semitic, Hamitic and Bantu. The first includes Arabic and Aethiopic; the last, a large number of languages south of the equator, the distinguishing characteristic of the group being the absence of gender inflexion, the use of nominal prefixes for the purpose of designating class, and the use of pronominal prefixes.

The second division, the Hamitic, was formerly treated as a subdivision of the Semitic, though it is now generally regarded as distinct from it. It includes Coptic, Berber and probably Hausa. Possibly the Hottentot languages of South Africa which, unlike the Bantu languages by which they are surrounded, possess a regular gender inflexion, bear some relation to this group.

M. Renan speaking of the limits of this group says:

'We must thus assign the Egyptian language and civilization to a distinct family, which we may call, if we will, Hamitic. To this same group belong doubtless the non-Semitic dialects of Abyssinia and Nubia. Future research will show whether, as has been conjectured, the indigenous languages to the north of Africa, the Berber and the Tuarek, for example, which appear to represent the Libyan and ancient Numidian, ought to be assigned to the same family.... It appears at any rate as the result of the latest explorations which have been made in Central Africa, that the Tuarek is simply Berber apart from Arabic influence, and that a distinct family of languages and peoples extends in Africa from the Egyptian oasis, and even from the Red Sea, to Senegal, and from the Mediterranean to the Niger' [1]).

Unfortunately no student either of Berber or of Coptic has as yet had the opportunity of studying Hausa. I am myself entirely ignorant of Coptic and possess only the most elementary knowledge of Berber.

The Berber language.

Before going on to speak of the structure of the Hausa language it will be well to say something in regard to the origin and spread of Berber.

The various dialects to which the name Berber has been given are spoken throughout the greater part of Africa north of the Sahara and west of and including Tripoli. They include the Tuarek, spoken on the borders of the great desert, the Kabyle spoken in Algeria,

---

[1]) *Histoire des langues sémitiques*, par Ernest Renan, I. 2. 89.

and Guanche, the language which was in use in the Canary Islands at the time of the Spanish conquest. The present Berber dialects are the descendants of the ancient Libyan or Numidian, which once prevailed throughout the whole of North Africa, to which S. Augustine referred when he wrote 'in Africa barbaras gentes in una lingua plurimas novimus'. The number of those who speak Berber in Algeria at the present time is 860,000. Berber is usually written in the Arabic characters, but traces of a distinctive alphabet are to be met with amongst certain of the Tuareks who speak a dialect called Tamáshek. This original alphabet, which bears no resemblance to Arabic, was probably at one time common to all the Berber dialects and was displaced when the introduction of Mohammedanism was followed by the introduction of the Koran and of the Arabic characters'.

The following points are of interest as tending to throw some light upon the connection between Hausa and Berber or other neighbouring languages.

The *genitive* in Hausa is usually denoted by *n* or *na*; thus 'the door of the house' would be *kofan gidda* or *kofa na gidda*. This method of forming the genitive is common to both Berber and Coptic.

Unlike most of the other languages, by which it is surrounded, Hausa possesses a regular *gender formation*, the general rule being that all words denoting the female sex and in addition all words ending in *a* are feminine. In one or two instances the Berber method of forming the feminine by prefixing a *t* is to be met with, thus *nágari* 'good' fem. *tágari*.

The *noun-agent* in Hausa is formed in a manner
closely resembling the Arabic viz. by prefixing *ma* or
mai to a verb, substantive, or adjective. Thus *gudu* is
to run, *maigudu* 'a fugitive'; *gidda* 'a house', *maigidda* 'the owner of a house'; *girima* 'great', *maigirima* 'a person who is great'.

In the Semitic languages proper the *verbal stem* undergoes a series of changes, by the addition of various
prefixes, by doubling one of the existing consonants,
or by modification of the vowel sounds. In this way
some fifteen voices or changes of meaning of a similar
character are obtained. In the Berber language there
are ten such voices, though the changes in the verbal
stem do not bear any close resemblance to those of
Arabic. There does not appear to be anything parallel
to this in the Fulah language which exists side by side
with Hausa in many parts of western Africa. In Hausa
there are apparently traces of four or five such changes, but with one exception, viz. the formation of the
passive voice, the changes in the sound of the words
do not correspond to any uniform changes of meaning.
The formation of the *passive voice* in Hausa bears a
striking resemblance to the VIIth form of the Arabic
or the Niphal of the Hebrew, both of which are used
in a middle or reflexive sense.

All the languages by which Hausa is surrounded, and
which I have been able to examine at all, form their
numerals with five as a base. In Berber the base was
originally five, though for numbers higher than four it
now employs numerals similar to the Arabic. In Fulah,
Bornuese and Nupé, the three most important languages

bordering on Hausa, the numerals are formed on a base of five; but except in the case of the higher numbers, which have been obviously borrowed within recent times from Arabic, they bear no resemblance to the Semitic numerals.

The numerals in Hausa are apparently formed on a base of ten, a fact which seems to prove that in very early times the Hausas were much more civilized than their neighbours, and which would also furnish an argument in favour of the supposition that the origin of Hausa is distinct from that of the surrounding languages. The Hausas possess an original system of enumeration from one to a thousand, though from twenty upwards numbers borrowed from Arabic are those most conmonly used. The number six *shidda* is the only one of the original numbers which at all resembles the Arabic.

The *personal pronouns* in Hausa with three exceptions, one of which *shi* 'he' has been apparently borrowed from the Bornuese, bear a close resemblance to the Arabic, a much closer resemblance moreover than they bear to the Berber. The rest of the pronouns in Fulah, and those in Nupé and Bornuese bear no resemblance to those in Hausa or in Arabic.

The only *coincidences between the Hausa and Coptic* vocabulary which I have been able to find are the Hausa *so* which, when connected with a numeral, means 'time' or 'times', cf. use of Coptic *sop*. The Hausa *fudu* 'four' seems to be the Coptic *ftu* and the Hausa *dubu* 'thousand' may perhaps be the Coptic *thba* meaning 'ten thousand'..

It does not seem possible to obtain any satisfactory

suggestion as to the *early habitat of the Hausa language*
from the names of its plants or animals. As regards the
names given to what must certainly have been introduced animals the evidence obtainable is singularly un-
satisfactory. There are several animals now common in
Hausaland which have been introduced within historical
time. We should naturally have expected that these
would be found to bear names similar to those which
they bore in their former home. Camels, horses, oxen
and sheep are all introduced animals; the former two
probably came across the desert by way of Bornu, the
latter two probably from the east by way of Darfur and
Wadai. In none of these four cases have I been able to
trace any connection between their Hausa names and
those which they bear in Arabic, Berber, or Bornuese.

Hausa has been reduced to writing for at least a century, and possibly very much longer. Native schools, in
which the children are taught to read and write, exist
throughout the whole of the country. The town of Kano,
which contains a population of about 120,000, has thirty
or forty schools. The literature existing in the country con-
sists chiefly of religious and warlike songs. Translations
from Arabic, histories and legal documents are also in
circulation. Despite the fact that the Hausa language is
spoken over such an enormous area, the difference between
its various dialects is very slight. In the town of Sokoto
the language has been influenced to a large extent by
the Fulah, which is spoken there as the court language,
but even a native of Sokoto seldom experiences any real
difficulty in making himself understood elsewhere.

Several of the sentences given in the exercises would

in actual conversation be further abbreviated, as the Hausas are fond of omitting words not absolutely necessary to convey the sense required.

In the case of the transliteration of many words a difficulty arises as to whether the consonant should be doubled or not. The sign of such doubling is nearly always omitted in written Hausa and in many words the pronunciation is by no means uniform, instances of this are *tafi* or *taffi* 'to go' *bisa* or *bissa* 'above' etc. etc.

In inserting references to, or quotations from, 'Specimens of Hausa Literature' I do not wish it to be inferred that any passage selected at random from the poems there reproduced can be relied upon as affording a standard of correct grammatical usage. In addition to a certain number of mistakes in transcription on the part of the native scribe, there are many mistakes of grammar, or at any rate inconsistent grammatical usages, in these poems.

The sign of reduplication of a consonant, called in Arabic *teshdid*, is more often omitted than inserted in Hausa. I have therefore omitted it as a general rule. When inserted it is usually written ـْ instead of ـّ as in Arabic.

Jezm ـْ or the sign used by the Arabs to show that a consonant is not accompanied by a vowel is usually employed by the Hausas. It is not inserted over a final ا or ى. The sign *hamza* ء which is employed by the Arabs to denote the cutting off of the stream of breath which can precede or follow a vowel, is but seldom employed in Hausa writing.

The Arabic signs *wasla* ٱ and *medda* ~, the first of which denotes that a vowel, the second that an ا has disappeared, are not used by the Hausas.

ALPHABET.

Names.	Unconnected	Connected only with the preceding	Connected on both sides	Connected only with the following	Pronunciation in Hausa.
اَلِڡ Alif	ا	ـا	. . .	. . .	
بَآ Ba	ب	ـب	ـبـ	بـ	English *b*.
تَآ Ta	ت	ـت	ـتـ	تـ	„ *t*.
ثَآ Cha	ث	ـث	ـثـ	ثـ	Soft *ch* as in *church*.
جِيم Jim	ج	ـج	ـجـ	جـ	English *j*.
حَآ Hha	ح	ـح	ـحـ	حـ	Strong *h*.
خَآ Kha	خ	ـخ	ـخـ	خـ	*kh* or hard *ch* as in Scotch *loch*.
دَال Dal	د	ـد	. . .	. . .	English *d*.
ذَال Zal	ذ	ـذ	. . .	. . .	„ *z*.
رَآ Ra	ر	ـر	. . .	. . .	„ *r*.
زَآ Za	ز	ـز	. . .	. . .	English *z*, pronounced the same as ذ.
سِين Sîn	س	ـس	ـسـ	سـ	English *s*.
شِين Shîn	ش	ـش	ـشـ	شـ	„ *sh*.
صَاد Sâd	ص	ـص	ـصـ	صـ	„ *s*, pronounced the same as س.
ضَاد Dâd	ض	ـض	ـضـ	ضـ	English *l*.
طَآ Ta	ط	ـط	ـطـ	طـ	„ *ts*, sometimes *t*.
ظَآ Tsa	ظ	ـظ	ـظـ	ظـ	English *ts*, very seldom used in Hausa.
عَين Ain	ع	ـع	ـعـ	عـ	

Names.	Unconnected	Connected only with the preceding	Connected on both sides	Connected only with the following	Pronunciation in Hausa.
غَيْن Ghain	غ	‍غ	‍غ‍	غ‍	English hard *g*.
بَآء Fa	ب	‍ب	‍ب‍	ب‍	English *f* (the dot is occasionally written above instead of below the letter as in Arabic).
قَاف Kâf	ف	‍ف	‍ف‍	ف‍	English *k* (this is occasionally written with two dots as in Arabic).
كَاف Kâf	ك	‍ك	‍ك‍	ك‍	*k*, pronounced the same as ف.
لَٱم Lâm	ل	‍ل	‍ل‍	ل‍	English *l*.
ميم Mîm	م	‍م	‍م‍	م‍	„ *m*.
نُون Nun	ن	‍ن	‍ن‍	ن‍	„ *n*.
هَآء Ha	ه	‍ه	‍ه‍	ه‍	*h*, pronounced the same as ح.
وَاو Wâ	و	‍و	. . .	. . .	English *w*.
يَآء Ya	ى	‍ى	‍ي‍	ي‍	„ *y*.

The vowel sounds in Hausa are ◌َ Fatha pronounced *a* or *e*; Kesre ◌ِ *i* or *e*; ◌ُ *u* or *o*. The Diphthongs are ◌َى *ai* pronounced as *i* in ice, ◌َو *au* pronounced *ow* as in cow.

The reader who is acquainted with Arabic will observe that ث and ض, which represent *th* and a sort of palatal *d* respectively in Arabic, are pronounced *ch* and *l* in Hausa.[1])

---

1) Cf. δάκρυ and lacryma, θώραξ and lorica; for parallel change in ancient Sanskrit cf. Whitney's Sanskrit Grammar §§ 53, 54.

The Arabic language contains several distinctions of
sound which are not found in Hausa at all. Thus no
clear distinction is recognized by the Hausas between
ز and ذ, س and ص, ف and ك, ح and ه, ل and ض
(this last letter is however very seldom used).

That no variation of sound is intended may be seen
from the fact that these letters are constantly interchanged. Compare غزری *gúzuri* F 67 and غذری *gúzuri*
F 68; غسكى *gaskia* B 66 and غصكى *gaṣkia* B 37;
بلول *fululu* C 36 and بضولوا *fuḷuluwa* B 154; كركتا
karkatta D 31 and كرفت *karḳatta* D 32; حم *himma*
for هم *ḥimma* E 42.

In transliterating Hausa into English I have represented the following letters thus ذ *ẓ*, ص *ṣ*, ف *ḳ*, ه *ḥ*,
ض *ḷ*. In each case the dot placed underneath the English letter does not represent any modification of sound.
For this reason I have omitted these dots altogether
in the first part of this grammar, in order to avoid
causing any unnecessary confusion to the beginner.

ف *ḳ* and ه *ḥ* are comparatively seldom used in Hausa;
most of the words in which they occur are borrowed
from Arabic.

The letters ١ and ع are used simply as the bearers
of the vowel sound. Thus the feminine personal pronoun
is spelt indifferently ١تا or عت; cf. A 14 and A 36,
in each case *ita* appears in the transliteration.

According to the general principle of transliteration
which I have adopted, an attempt has been made to
reproduce the sound of the words rather than to reproduce
duce each separate letter of the original, as to do both

was impossible. Had I transliterated each separate letter much unnecessary confusion would have been caused, the confusion being due to the lack of uniformity of transcription adopted by the Hausa scribe.

In a few instances I have placed an accent over a vowel in order to indicate that the emphasis falls on a particular syllable. As however this emphasis differs a good deal in different localities I have made but sparing use of such.

PRONUNCIATION.

The following is a more complete account of the pronunciation of the English letters used in transliterating Hausa.

Letters	Pronunciation
a	*a* as in *father*.
b	as in English.
ch	soft *ch* as in *church* or *cherry*.
d	as in English.
e	as *a* in *fate*.
f	as in English.
g	hard *g* as in *gate*, never soft as in *genius*.
h	as in English, always pronounced if inserted.
i	as *i* in *ravine*, or as *ee* in *feet*.
j	as in English.
k	„ „ „
kh	a rough form of the

Letters	Pronuncitation
	Scotch *ch* in *loch*. It resembles the sound made in trying to raise something in the throat.
l m n	as in English.
o	*o* as in *mote*.
p	as in English. In Hausa *p* and *b* both appear as *b*; the sounds are frequently interchanged.
r s sh	as in English.

Letters	Pronunciation	Letters	Pronunciation
t	as in English.		used except as a consonant.
u	*u* as in *flute*, or *oo* as in *tool*.	*z*	as in English.
w	*w* as in *win*.	*ai*	as *i* in *ice*.
y	*y* as in *yard*. It is never	*au*	as *ow* in *how*.

The general rules of the system of transliteration are:

a. all consonants are pronounced as in English.

b. all vowels are pronounced as in Italian.

c. all vowels are shortened in sound by doubling the following consonant.

According to the above system, which is that originally propounded by the Royal Geographical Society, an approximation to the sound is alone aimed at. Neither the English nor the Arabic alphabet is at all perfectly adapted to express the inflections of sound and accent, which can be acquired only from direct intercourse with the natives.

PRONOUNS.

LESSON I.

The following are the Personal Pronouns which would be used to answer the question, who?

	Sing.	*Plur.*
I pers.	*ni*	*mu*
II pers. {m.	*kai*	*ku*
f.	*ki*	
III pers. {m.	*shi*	*su*
f.	*ita*	

The oblique cases of the personal pronouns are expressed by the following suffixes.

	Sing.	*Plur.*
I pers.	*ni*	*mu*
II pers. {m.	*ka*	*ku*
f.	*ki*	
III pers. {m.	*shi, sa*	*su*
f.	*ta*	

Examples, *ya gansu* 'he saw them', *ta ganka* 'she saw you', *su hawa doki* 'they mounted the horse'.

The forms *na, ka, ki, ya, ta, mu, ku, su,* when used with the verbal stem, which itself remains unaltered, denote the Aorist, or Indefinite tense.

To express negation *ba* is placed before and after either the verb or the whole statement negatived. Thus we may say either *ba ya gani ba mutum*, or more commonly, *ba ya gani mutum ba*, 'he did not see the man'; *ba* followed by the first personal pronoun is written *ban*.

There is no word in Hausa to denote *interrogation*; it is usually expressed by a change in the intonation. When it is desired to emphasize the interrogative character of the sentence the words *ko ba hakka ba* lit. 'or is it not so', are frequently added; this again is often shortened into *ko*. In the case of a negative interrogation the second *ba* is often omitted.

There is no *article* in Hausa. Thus *mutum* means 'man', 'a man', or 'the man'.

mutum pl. *mutane* man.	*machi* woman.
babu nothing.	*hakka* thus or so.
sanu sanu very slowly (lit. slowly slowly).	*massa massa* very quickly (lit. quickly, quickly).
taffi or *tafi* to go.	*ga* or *gani* to see.
amma but.	*a* or *aa* no.
yaro boy.	*yarinia* girl.
ko or.	*doki* horse.
hawa to mount (a horse).	*yi* to do or to make.

EXERCISE I.

ka gani machi ko yarinia. yaro ya taffi massa massa amma yarinia ta taffi sanu sanu. mutum ya hawa doki ya taffi. ba ka gani doki ba. yarinia ta hawa doki ta taffi massa. mutum ba ya yi hakka ba amma machi ta yi hakka.

Did the boy mount the horse? No, but the man

mounted, the boy did not do so, he went away very
quickly. Did the man go away very slowly, or did he
not? No, he went away very slowly. I did not do so.
Did not the woman see the horse?

LESSON II.

The Possessive Pronouns are:

	Separable.		Inseparable.
	When object possessed is *masculine*.	When object possessed is *feminine*.	
1. P. M.	*nawa*	*tawa*	-*na*
F.	*nata* [1])	*tata* [1])	-*nta*, -*ta*
2. P. M.	*naka*	*taka*	-*nka*, -*ka*
F.	*naki*	*taki*	-*nki*, -*ki*
3. P. M.	*nasa*	*tasa*	-*nsa*,-*sa*, -*nshi*,-*shi*
F.	*nata*	*tata* [1])	-*nta*, -*ta*
1. P.	*namu*	*tamu*	-*nmu*, -*mu*
2. P.	*naku*	*taku*	-*uku*, -*ku*
3. P.	*nasu*	*tasu*	-*nsu*, -*su*

The above table is constructed on the following system; the first element *na* m. or *ta* f. agrees in gender
with the thing possessed, the second agrees in gender
with the possessor. The inseparable pronouns agree in
gender with the possesseor.

Examples, 'my father', if the speaker were a man,
would be, *uba nawa* or *ubana*; if the speaker were a
woman, it would be, *uba nata* or *ubata*; 'my mother',
if the speaker were a man, would be, *uwa tawa* or

---

1) These forms are rarely used, *nawa*, *tawa*, *tasa*, being used instead.

2

uwana, if the speaker were a woman, it would be, *uwa tata* [1]) or *uwata*.

The above system appears to be too elaborate even for the Hausas themselves to observe. In conversation, and sometimes in writing too, masculine forms are substituted for feminine; thus we have *almajinka* for *almajinki* 'thy husband'. D. 52.

Reflexive and emphatic forms of the Pronouns are formed by the use of the words *da kai*, lit. 'with the head'. Thus *ni dakaina* 'I myself', *kai dakanka, ki dakanki, shi dakansa* etc. These forms are sometimes abbreviated to *kaina, kanka* etc.

Kaddai or *kadai* 'only' is also used to add emphasis to the Personal Pronouns: thus *ni kaddai* 'I indeed'.

rua water.	*chikkin* or *achik-kin* in or into.	*kofa* door.
rijia a well.		*jibi* the day after tomorrow.
yo today.	*gidda* house.	
gata three days hence.	*gobi* tomorrow.	*watan jia* last month (lit. month of yesterday.
wata month.	*watan yo* this-month (lit. month of today).	
jia yesterday		*gari* place, or town.
shekaranjia the day before yesterday.	*fada* or *fadda* to speak *che* to say.	
	fadda. to fight	*fada* to fall.
ga, or *gare* to.	*mi* or *mine ni* what?	*don* (conj.) that or because.
ba or *bada* to give.	*a* or *aa* no.	
	enna where?	

gare usually implies motion towards; it is used with the

---

1) These forms are rarely used, *nawa, tawa, tasa*, being used instead.

personal pronouns where *ga* would be used with nouns.
da ya issa enough (lit. that which is sufficient).

EXERCISE II.

mi ya faḍa maka yaro? ya che rua ba ya issa
ba chikkin giddansa. machi ta taffi yo ko jia? aa ,ta
taffi shekaranjia. kakka kofan giddamu ta fada? ni da
kaina ban sani ba amma kai ka sani. mi ka gani chikkin
gari? na gani rijia amma babu rua chikinta. kai yaro
fadda mani abin da machi ta che maka. ban ganta ¹) ba.

The boy says that the man himself gave him the
horse. The house is ours, not yours. Give me water, because there is not enough in the town. We have none
ourselves, but go to my house in the town, and say to
our boy 'give me water'. I went to your house, but the
boy says that there is not enough water in your well.
What did the man say to you? I did not see ¹ him
in the house.

LESSON III.

The *Demonstrative* Pronouns are:

	Fem.	*Plural.*	
wonan ²)		*woddanan* or	
		wodanan	
wonga	*wogga*	*wodanga*	this near by.
nan			
-nga			
wonchan	*wochan*	*woddanan*	that over there.

---

1) The final *i* in *gani* 'to see' is usually omitted before the personal
pronouns.

2) *Wonan wodanan wodanga* are often written in Hausa *wanan wa-
danan wadanga* but are generally pronounced as above.

-nga (which, especially in the northern part of Hausaland is sometimes written *-lga,*) is only used after a noun ending in a vowel, thus *kofanga* 'this door'. *nan* and *nga* follow the noun to which they are attached, *wonan, wonga* and *wonchan* usually precede it; thus, *wonan litafi* or *litafi nan* 'this book'; *nan* is also used as an adverb meaning 'here'. In Sokoto and the western parts of Hausaland *worga* or *warga* is often used instead of *wonga* and *wogga. wonan* .... *wonan* is equivalent to 'this .... that'; thus, *ina so wonan ba wonan* 'I like this, not that'.

The *Relative* Pronouns are *woni* and *wonda,* who, which; *wonda* has a feminine form *woda* or *wodda,* and they both use as a plural *wodanda* or *woddanan; wonda* and *woddanda* are very frequently abbreviated into *nda* or *da;* thus, *abin da kana so* 'that which you want' *garinda ka gani* 'the place which you saw'.

The *noun-agent* in Hausa is formed in a manner closely resembling the Arabic, viz, by prefixing *mai* to a verb, substantive, or adjective. Thus *gudu* 'to run', *maigudu* 'a fugitive'; *gidda* 'a house' *maigidda* 'the owner of the house'; *girima* 'great' *maigirima* 'a person who is great'. The plural of such words is formed by changing *mai* into *masu,* thus *masugudu* 'fugitives'.

ma is used similarly as a verbal prefix; thus, *saki* 'to weave', *masaki* pl. *masaka* 'a weaver'. It is also used to denote place or agent; thus, *karatu* 'to read', *makaranta* 'a school'; *sabka* 'to unload', *masabki* 'a lodging'.

The *substantive Verb* 'to be' is expressed by *ni, ki*

chi, (or *che*) the last form being usually employed when the preceding word is feminine. The verb 'to be' is however almost as often omitted as expressed; thus, *ita machi ba miji ba* 'it is a woman, not a man'.

koma to go back.	*koiya* to teach.	*zaki* lion.
komo to come back.	*koiyo* to learn.	*jaki* ass.
dawoiyo or *dawoyo* to return here.	*chiniki* trade, bartering.	*idan* or *en* if.
dawoiya or *dawoya* to return to a place at a distance.	*yi chiniki* to do business.	*tari da* together with.
kawo to bring.	*kurdi* money, price.	*yaka* come!
		dagga from.

EXERCISE III.

maijaki ba shi so shi dawoiyo ba don ba shi sonka ba. yarona shika koiyo babu don makoiyo nasa ya bershi chikkin gari. kai yaro' yaka zan baka kurdi. mutum nan shi ni maigidda amma giddansa ta fada. wonan machi chi wodda kana so ko ba hakka ba? zaki chan da ka gani ya taffi massa massa. mairijianga ya kawo rua dagga rijiansa. zan dawoiyo gareka gobi.

If you wish to barter for the ass, come to my house to-morrow. Where is the owner of this horse, tell him that if he leaves it here, it will go back to the town. This teacher says that the boy whom you brought with you does not wish to learn. If you wish to come with me, we will go into the town and barter with the traders there. The owner of my house has gone away, his boy says that he will not return till the day after to-morrow.

LESSON IV.

The *Interrogaiive* Pronouns are:

    wa or *wane* f. *wache* pl. *sua* who, which, what?

    nwa whose?

    waneni pl. *suaneni* who?

    mi, *mine*, or *mineni* what?

    nawa how much?

The suffixes *ne che* are the M. and F. forms of the verb 'to be'; thus *waneni* is properly 'who is it'? *waneni kai* 'who. are you'?

In Interrogative sentences the personal pronoun is used before the verb as well as the Interrogative pronoun thus; *wa ya fada maka labári* 'who told you the news? *mi ya sameka* 'what is the matter with you'? *tumkia-nwa ke nan* ' whose sheep is this'? *suaneni* is chiefly used in the sentence *suaneni nι* for 'who are they'?

Nia is used, especially in Sokoto, to ask the question 'is it I'?

The *Indefinite* Pronouns most of which are formed from the Interrogative by prefixing the particle *ko*, are:

    kowa everyone, anyone, any.

    kowani (or *kowaneni*) f. *kowachi* (or *kowoni* f. *kowo-*
        chi) a strengthened form of *kowa*.

    komi or *komine* everything, anything.

    woni (or *wonni*) f. *wota* pl. *wonsu*, *wosu* or *woddansu*
        someone, something, a certain person or thing;
        the plural often means, others, *woui ... woni* de-
        notes, the one ... the other.

babu kowa, or *ba kowa*, or *babu wonda*, no one.

babu komi or *ba komi ba*, nothing.

kowani is combined with the plural of the personal pronoun; thus, *kowanemu* 'each of us', *kowanenku* 'each of you', *kowanensu* 'each of them'.

The following are examples of *Reciprocal Pronouns*, formed by prefixing *juna* to the plurals of the personal pronouns, thus *junamu*, *junanku*, *junansu* 'one another'; *juna* is also used by itself, in which case it is usually pronounced *jiuna*; thus, *ba su iya wuchi jiuna* 'they were not able to pass each other'.

Reflexive Pronouns are formed by means of *kai* or *dakai* as explained in Lesson II.

Tunkuda to push or butt.   *tumkia* pl. *tumaki* sheep.

iri kind, sort.   *tsuntsua* bird.

bako a stranger.

EXERCISE IV.

mutum nan ya che ba shi sani ba wonda ya kawo kurdi. kadda ka fada labari ga (*or* ma) kowa. woni mutum ya hawa doki woni ya hawa jaki. kowachi yarinia tana da uwa. kai yaro yaka mi ya sameka? babu komi. woni irin tsuntsua ki nan? wodansu mutane suna koiyo massa massa wodansu ba iya koiyo komi ba. kowani mutum shina so kansa. tumaki suna tunkuda junansu.

The men returned each to their own house. Some men came to my house yesterday, but I do not know who they were. Do not tell that which I told you to any one in the town. This man told me that he was a stranger and that no one here knew him; he came

with a certain man whom I knew, the day before yesterday. What kind of door do you like in your house?

THE VERB.

LESSON V.

The *Aorist* or *Indefinite* tense of the Verb is formed
by prefixing to the verbal stem the simplest forms of
the Personal Pronouns as given in Lesson I.

The *Future* tense of the verb is formed by prefixing
za to the pronouns as given in Lesson I with a slight
modification in the II and III pers. Thus the future of
yi 'to make' is

Sing.	*Plural.*
1. *zani* (or *zan*) *yi*	1. *zamu yi*
2. *zaka yi*	2. *zaku yi*
f. *zaki yi*	
3. *zashi yi*	3. *zasu yi*
f. *zata yi.*	

The word *da* is used in Hausa in several different
senses.

1. as a preposition or conjunction meaning 'and',
   'with', or 'when'.
2. as the verb 'to have' or 'to possess'. Ex. *suna
   da bindigogi* 'they have guns'.
3. it is used, when combined with substantives, to
   form adjectives. Thus we have *rai* 'life' *da rai*
   'alive', *anfani* 'use' *da anfani* 'useful', *yungwa*
   'hunger' *da yungwa* 'hungry'.

4. as a relative pronoun meaning 'which', especially in the expression *abin da* 'the thing which' Ex. *zan yi abin da ka che* 'I will do what you say'.

There are, moreover, three other words; *da* or *daa* 'of old', *da* 'son,' and *da* 'free,' Ex. *ni da ni ba bawa ba* 'I am free, not a slave'.

Sai is used in the following senses:

1. meaning 'only', 'except', or 'but', thus *sai wonan* 'only this'.

2. meaning 'until' *sai ka tsofi* '(wait) till you grow old' B. 115. *sai gobi* 'until tomorrow'.

3. in salutations *sai lafia* 'hail'!

akoi there is or there are.	*dagga enna* whence?	*ba gaskia* to speak the truth.
abin thing pl. *abu* or *abubua*.	*yanzu* now. *taffo* to come.	*fito* or *fitto* to come out from.
abin da which, or what	*gaskia* truth. *da gaskia* true or	*fita* or *fitta* to go out from.
enna where?	truly.	*bata* destroyed, or
dagga from?		to be destroyed.
zo to come.		

EXERCISE V.

dagga enna mutum nan ya taffo. ya fada mani ya fito dagga kano. ban sani ba abin da zamu yi yanzu. yaro nan ya che shina da yungwa amma mu dakaimu ba muna da abinchi. mata chan ta che ba zata taffi ba sai mu zo. gidda taka enna anfaninta? tana bata. ban sani ba enna kofa na giddanga. en ba ka bani gaskia ba zan taffi. abinda ka bani shekaranjia ba shi da anfani. mutum nan ba zashi fadda ba don bindigansa ta bata.

The man whom you saw yesterday has come. He says that he will tell you the truth now, if you will see him. Tell him that I will not see him till to-morrow, because it is of no use to day. There is no man here who speaks the truth. Is that man alive or not? It is of no use to say this to me, because I know that it is not so. Give me something to eat for I am hungry, I ate nothing yesterday on the day before. I will not give you anything to eat till to-morrow. What is the use of this man? he will not fight because his gun is destroyed. I will give him a gun in order that he may go out and fight.

LESSON VI.

The *Present* tense is formed by adding *na* to the simple forms of the personal pronouns as given in Lesson I. The first person singular does not take an additional *na*.

The *Perfect* tense is formed by means of the following pronominal prefixes:

Sing.	Plural.
1. *nika* or *nina*	1. *muka*
2. *kaka* f. *kika*	2. *kuka*
3. *shika* f. *taka*	3. *suka*.

The *Passive Voice* is formed by prefixing *a an ana aka* or *anka* to the Active form. The first three prefixes are used for the present, the last two for the past tense of the Passive. When the passive form is used, the pronouns are placed after the verb thus *kasshe* is 'to kill', *anakasshe* 'to be killed', *akasshesu* or *anakas-shesu* 'they are killed', *akakasshesu* 'they have been killed'. When *kadda* precedes the simple forms of the personal pronouns, it has the force of a prohibition; thus, *kadda ka yi hakka* 'do not do so'. *kadda* is also used in the sense of 'lest'. Thus *na ji tsoro kadda su kassheni* 'I fear lest they may kill me'.

The forms of the *Imperative* are the same as in the past tense of the Indicative; thus, *ka bani wonan* may be either, 'give me this' or 'you gave me this'. Occasionally the pronoun is omitted altogether in the Imperative; thus, *bani wonan* 'give me this'.

In the Passive voice the Imperative forms are the same as the Indicative, but the final pronoun is usually omitted, thus *akakawo* 'let it be brought'.

karia false or falsehood.	*bawa* slave.	*rakumi* camel.
rago ram.	*kussa* or *kusa* near.	*nesa* or *da nesa* far.
bissa or *bisa* above.	*kalkashin* below, under.	*kuma* again.
mugu bad.	*tsoro* fear.	*dadi* sweet.
ji to feel.	*ji tsoro* to be afraid.	*ji dadi* to be happy.
ber or *berri* to leave or allow.	*so* to love, to wish.	*abinshi* anything to eat.
abinsha anything to drink.	*akass* (for *a kasa*) on the ground.	*garin* on account of.
		gudu or *guddu* to run.

EXERCISE VI.

mutum wonda ga kasshe rakumina shi ya yi abin mugu. kadda ka berri rakumi naka don zashi gudu. mutane nan suka chi ragonsu su ji dadi yanzu. yaro

shika hawa bissa rakumin ubansa amma ya fada akass.
ina so en taffi nesa dagga gari nan don ban sonsa. kai
bawa taffo kusa gareni kadda ka ji tsoro ba zani chika
ba. rago chan ba shina da abinchi ba. kadda ka bershi
hakka. yaro kadda ka taffi da nesa ina sonka. na ji tsoro
garin rago nan don ya taffi kusa ga rijia kadda shi
fáda chikinta.

Do not let your boy mount my camel lest he fall.
Give me water from the well in your house, for I have
nothing now to drink. Tell the man that if he comes
to see me to-morrow, I will not see him. These men
have told me lies, they do not wish to speak the truth.
If the ram has been killed, do not let the men eat it
now, because when they have eaten it they will not wish
to go far. What shall we do now? Do not go away, or
leave us till we feel happy again. Do not be afraid, we
will not leave you.

LESSON VII.

There are two *numbers* in Hausa, singular and plural.
The plural of nouns is formed in a large number of
different ways [1]. In the case of words ending in *a* the
plural is formed:

1. By changing the final *a* into *i*, *ai*, or *u*.
2. by adding *ni*, *ki*, or *yi* to the singular.
3. By changing the final *a* into *o*, reduplicating the
   last syllable and adding *i*.
4. By changing the final *a* into *u* and adding *na*.
5. By adding *shi* to the singular.

---

1) There are moreover very many words which conform to no appa-
rent rule.

The following are examples of the above rules.

Sing.	Plur.	Sing.	Plur.
1. *hankaka*	*hankaki* quail.	3. *yasa*	*yasosi* finger.
alura	*alurai* needle.	*fuska*	*fuskoki* face.
dorina	*dorinai* hippo-	*tufa*	*tufofi* clothes.
	potamus.	4. *sanda*	*sanduna* stick.
aljifa	*aljifu* small	*riga*	*riguna* garment.
	bag, pocket.	*ganga*	*ganguna* drum.
shekkara	*shekkaru* year ¹)5.	*gidda*	*giddaji* or *giddashi*
	(or *shekara-u*).		house.
2. *uba*	*ubani* father.	*bissa*	*bissashi* beast.
kwana	*kwanaki* day.	*kuda*	*kudaji* or *kudashi*
gona	*gonaki* farm.		fly.
uwa	*uwayi* mother.	*kasa*	*kasashi* earth,
giwa	*giwayi* elephant.		land.

nawa how much,   *domi* why?
or how many?
chika full, or to fill.   *tataka* to tread down.   *zua* coming.

EXERCISE VII.

gonakinsa suna da nesa dagga gari en na taffi chan
dorina zashi chini. enna maisanduna nan ya taffi? ya
beri sanduna nasa ya taffi gonansa. akoi gidda kusa da
gonansa ko ba hakka ba? akoi. gidda anyi da sanduna
amma ita ta bata yanzu don giwayi suka tatakata. nawa
alurai kana chikkin aljifanka? idan ka fada chikkin

---

1) The examples given under this rule may perhaps be the result of
a reduplication of the last syllable (cf. L. VIII, 2); the plural forms
would thus have originally been *giddadi*, *bissasi*, *kudadi*, *kasasi*.

rijia nan zaka bata riganka don tana chika da rua. ganga nan mineni kurdinsa? (*or* enna kurdin ganga?) ban sanni ba amma maiganga dakansa shina zua. akoi gonaki diawa achikkin kano amma giddashi duka ba su da gonaki kusa garesu ba.

Go with my slave to the town, and ask the owner of these drums what the price of these drums is, and if he wishes to sell them. He says that he will not tell me the price, but that if you will come to the town, he will bargain with you yourself. Your camel has eaten my clothes, I do not know what to do. It is not my camel who has eaten your clothes; it is the camel of the man who went away from here yesterday. If I come with you to your house, I am afraid lest the elephants should come and tread down my farm. Do not be afraid, my boy will not allow them to come near or to tread it down.

LESSON VIII.

The *plural* of nouns ending in *i* is formed:

1. By changing the final *i* into *a*, or *ai*.
2. By changing the final *i* into *a* and reduplicating the last syllable.
3. By changing the final *i* into *una*, or *ayi*.

In the case of words ending in *e* the plural is formed

4. By changing the final *e* into *ayi*.
5. By irregular reduplication.

The following are examples of the above rules

Sing.	Plur.		Sing.	Plur.	
1. *rakumi*	*rakuma*	camel.	3. *daki*	*dakuna*	room.
takalmi	*takalma*	shoe.	*surdi*	*surduna*	saddle.
aboki	*abokai*	friend.	*kifi*	*kifayi*	fish.
machiji	*machijai*	snake.	*biri*	*birayi*	monkey.
2. *iri*	*irari*	nation, seed, kind.	4. *fure*	*furayi*	a flower.
wuri	*wurari*	place.	5. *karre*	*karnuka*	dog.

kasua market.
duka all every.
kai to carry.
iya to be able.

ya kamata it is necessary, or it is right.
sayi or *saida* to buy.

sayes or *sayesda* to sell.
dilali trade, broker.
yi dilali to trade.

EXERCISE VIII.

mineni irin (*or* wonni irin) birayi akoi chikkin kasan hausawa? birayi da ni na gani suna da fuskoki kaman karnuka. akoi kifayi chikin kasuan kano, ka iya-n-fada mani dagga enna masuchiniki su kawosu. kifayi duka da ka saidasu dagga mutane nan ankawosu dagga nesa. idan kana da takalma ba ya kamata ba kana jin tsoron machijai. masudilalin surduna nan ba suna da gaskia ba, ba zan yi chiniki da su ba. kai abokina ka taffi kasua ka tambaia mairakumi nan enna kurdinsa. akoi furayi diawa chikkin gonanka, ina so ka kawosu ga gidda, zan yi chiniki.

If you want to buy a camel, you must go to those who sell them in the market. I have been there, but I cannot do business with those who sell them, because they will not tell me their price, and if they do tell it me they do not speak the truth. Ask my friend to go with you, he knows all who sell in the market, they cannot tell lies to him. What sort of shoes do you wish to buy. I want all the kinds that you have with you to-day. If you buy shoes from that man, they will soon be destroyed, and you will not be able to travel far. It is not necessary that you should carry your shoes into the market, you can leave them here.

LESSON IX.

The *plural* of nouns ending in *o* is formed:

1. By changing the final *o* into *a* or *i*.
2. By changing the *o* into *ayi*, *una* or *anu*.
3. By adding *ni* or *ri* to the singular.

In the case of words ending in *u* the plural is formed
4. By adding *a* or *na* to the singular.

Almost any noun can be used collectively, and construed as though it were plural; thus we may say either *mutum biu* or *mutane biu* 'two men'. Many nouns use two or even three different forms of the plural; thus the plural of *kai* 'head' is *kanua*, *kauna* or *kawuna*; of *sariki* 'king' *sarikai* or *sarakuna*.

It will be noticed that as a general rule dissyllables add a syllable in the plural; words of more than two syllables seldom do so.

The following are examples of the above rules.

Sing.	Plur.		Sing.	Plur.
1. *yaro*	*yara, yarayi* or *ya-yayi*, boy.		*rago*	*raguna* a ram.
kafo	*kafi* blind.		*kwado*	*kwaduna* or *kwa-dodi* toad or frog.
tsofo	*tsofi* old person.		*ido*	*idanu* eye.
2. *gado*	*gaday*i or *gadoji*, hog.	3.	*kafo*	*kafoni* horn.
			taro	*tarori* multitude, abundance.
gado	*gadaji* bed.			
rago	*ragayi* an idle person.	4.	*hanu*	*hanua* hand.
			taru	*taruna* net.

worigi play.	*fara, faruna* or	*chiawa* grass.
yi worigi to play.	*farori* locust.	*daa* or *lokachin*
kara (m.) reed or reeds.	*daffa* to cook.	*daa* in olden time.
maibarra or *mai-roko* a beggar.	*dummi* or *dumi* noise.	*wuta* fire.
		nema to search for.

EXERCISE IX.

chikkin kano akoi taron kafi daia tsakansu sunansa sarikin kafi. kafi diawa su zo kasua neman kurdi ko abinchi wurin masusayi ko masusayes. naman gadoji ba ya kamata ba ka chishi amma naman raguna ka iya ka chishi. dakuna nawa akoi chikkin giddanka? akoi sai daia amma ina so en gina daki woni kuma. karnuka ba su yi komi da rana amma da derri ba su kwana ba suna so suna gudu ko suna yi worigi: kwadodi suna so wurin da akoi rua diawa, idan ka taffi nemansu ba ka iya ganesu ba. raguna achikkin. kano suna da kafoni, amma wosu ba suna da kafoni ba.

The Hausas catch locusts with nets, they like to cook

and eat them. The frogs make a great noise during the night, they like to stay in the grass near the water. How is a bed made in the country of the Hausas? There are two sorts of beds, one is made with mud, and the other with reeds. If the bed is made with mud, a place for a fire is made underneath it. You can buy beds made of reeds in the market-place. From what place did the Hausas come in olden time? They say that they came from the town of Daura, but if you ask them whence they came before they lived in Daura, they will tell you that they came from a place far away beyond Mecca. Kano is the name of the king who built the town, the name of which is now Kano.

LESSON X.

The Hausa language, unlike many of the languages by which it is surrounded, possesses a distinct *gender formation*. Many of these languages know of no distinction except that existing in nature, which is as a rule expressed by a totally distinct word. Hausa possesses two genders, masculine and feminine. All words which denote the female sex are feminine, and in addition nearly all words in the language ending in *a*. The feminine sex is denoted by various modifications of the masculine termination. Thus

masc.	*fem.*	*masc.*	*fem.*
karre dog.	*karria* bitch.	*gado* pig.	*gadonia* sow.
yaro boy.	*yarinia* girl.	*sariki* king.	*saraunia* queen.
kane younger brother.	*kanua* younger sister.	*da* son.	*dia* daughter.
		sa bull.	*sania* cow.

masc.	fem.	masc.	fem.
bara servant.	*barania.*	*bara* servant.	*barania.*
babe locust.	*babania.*	*tsofo* old man.	*tsofua.*
barao thief.	*baraunia.*		

There are a few feminines which do not end in *a*, and are not used to denote distinction of sex, e. g. *zani* 'cloth', *safe* 'early morning'. The word *itachi*, if treated as masculine, denotes 'a tree'; if as feminine, it denotes 'a branch cut from a tree'.

The gender of a considerable number of words is uncertain, some natives regarding them as masculine, others as feminine, e. g. *hainya* 'road'. *hainya ta budi* 'the road is open'.

gurubin instead of.   *ji mamaki* to wonder.
yi daria to laugh.   *nama* flesh.
yi mamaki to make to wonder.

EXERCISE X.

yaro ya fi yarinia da karifi amma ba ya fita ba da anfani. mutani duka chikkin kasan hausa su ji mamaki don muna da saraunia gurubin sariki chikin kasamu, su yi daria koyaushi da na fada masu hakka. idan kana so en fura wuta ya kamata ka doka itachin wuta da ta fada kalkashin itachi amma ba ya kamata ba ka yenki itachi dakansa. baraunia ta taffi da rago da na kawa, ba ni da abinchi ba. kana so ka bani rago gurubin taruna?

In the market of Kano the flesh of the bull and the cow are sold. If you wish to buy it, you must go to the market in the early morning. In the country at a

distance from the towns not many ·people eat beef, because they are not able to get it. The Hausas wonder
at strangers who come into their country, because they
eat much meat. The dogs come into the towns at night,
and they eat everything which men do not care to eat,
and which is left outside the houses. The dogs are on
this account of much use. If you look for flowers, all
the Hausas will wonder what you are doing, they
themselves do not care for flowers.

LESSON XI.

The distinction between the two genders is often
made by using two quite distinct words. This is especially common where the distinction between the two
genders exists in nature.

The distinction between the genders is also frequently
expressed by using either as prefixes or suffixes *namiji*
or *miji* 'male' and *machi* 'female'.

uba father.	*uwa* mother.
wa elder brother.	*ya* elder sister.
miji or *namiji* man.	*machi* woman.
rakumi camel.	*tagua* female camel.
bunsuru he-goat.	*akwia* she-goat. (pl. *awaki*.)
doki horse. (pl. *dawaki*).	*godia* mare.
sarmayi youth.	*budurua* maid.
toro male elephant.	*giwa* female elephant.
alfadari mule.	*hakkorin giwa* ivory.
halbi to shoot.	*kibia* arrow. (pl. *kibo*.)
deffi poison.	

There are no modifications of substantives for the
sake of expressing Cases. The Genitive is usually ex-

pressed by the use of the preposition *na* 'of'; this is generally contracted into *n*. The genitive is moreover often expressed simply by apposition; thus we may say *kofa na gidda*, *kofan gidda*, or *kofa gidda* 'the door of the house.' In this particular instance the second form would be that most commonly used. In the case of feminine words *ta* is used instead of *na* thus, *akwia ta bako* 'the stranger's she-goat'.

EXERCISE XI.

ko rakumi ko tagua ka fiso? na fiso rakumi don ya fi tagua da karifi. ina tamaha godia ta fi doki da anfani. godia ba ta yi fushi kaman doki, achikkin kasua kurdinta ya fi kurdin doki, ko? aa ba ya fi ba. mutani diawa suna tamaha alfadari ya fi su biu don wonan alfadara diawa asayesu chikkin kasua. dilali ya che ba shi so ba en baka doki gurubin alfadari naka don ya fiso dokinsa. maidoki ya che zashi baka dawaki biu gurubin bawanka. aa na fiso bawana.

Tell me how the Hausas kill elephants in their country in order to take the ivory. They see the places where the elephants come to drink at night, then they ascend a tree near, and when the elephant comes to drink, they shoot arrows with poison on them. The elephant is not able to see the man, and is frightened. When it runs away, the man comes down from the tree and runs behind it, and does not leave it till the elephant falls down and dies. The elephant can run very fast. If a man comes near to it, it will kill him. It is not afraid of men.

LESSON XII.

The *cardinal numbers* up to a hundred are as follows:

1. *daia.*	13. *goma sha uku.*
2. *biu.*	20. *ashirin* or *ishirin.*
3. *uku.*	21. *ashirin da daia.*
4. *fudu* sometimes pro-	22. *ashirin da biu.*
nounced *hudu.*	30. *tallatin.*
5. *biar, bial* or *biat.*	31. *tallatin da daia.*
6. *shidda.*	40. *arbaïn.*
7. *bokkoi.*	50. *hamsin.*
8. *tokkos.*	60. *settin.*
9. *tara.*	70. *sebbaïn.*
10. *goma.*	80. *tamanin.*
11. *goma sha daia.*	90. *tissaïn.*
12. *goma sha biu.*	100. *dari, zango,* or *mia.*

In the case of the numbers 11 to 19 inclusive the word *goma* is omitted in ordinary conversation, thus 13 would be simply *sha uku*. The two numbers just below the decades are expressed by using *babu* 'nothing' or 'not'; thus 19 would be *ashirin daia babu*, 29 *tallatin daia babu*, 38 *arbaïn biu babu* etc.

hauïa twenty is often used in counting cowries for numbers divisible by twenty; thus, 40 would be *hauia biu*, 60 *hauia uku* etc., *lasso* is also occasionally used, for 20. *gomia* a plural form of *goma* is sometimes used for expressing the decades above 10; thus, 20 would be *gomia biu*, 30 *gomia uku*. *zango* or *zungo* usually denotes 100 cowries.

The arabic numerals *talata* 3, *arbaa* 4, *hamsa* 5,

etc. are frequently used to express 3000, 4000, 5000 etc. *dubu* being understood.

da tsada dear.

da araha cheap.

[1]) *kwana* pl. *kwanaki* day.

wuri pl. *kurdi* cowry.

jaki pl. *jakuna* donkey.

issa to arrive at, to be equal to.

wonni which?

shekara or *shekkara* pl.

shekaru year.

kuddus south.

berchi to sleep.

kwoi egg or eggs.

tun or *tunda* till, since, now.

haifua birth.

kaffa foot, leg.

a kaffa on foot.

EXERCISE XII.

kai yaro shekarunka nawa? (*or* shekara nawa kana da rai, *or* shekara nawa tun haifuanka) skekarana yanzu ta yi kusa sha bokkoi amma kanena shekaransa sai sha daia. kwanaki nawa dagga bida zua kano? mutùm maidoki ya issa bida dagga kano kwanaki goma sha fudu amma mutum a kaffa ba zashi fito ba sai kwanaki ashirin ko ashirin da biu. wonni ya fi tsada ko doki ko rakumi? achikkin kano doki ya fi rakumi da araha amma rakuma ba su iya ba su taffi kuddus da nesa dagga kano. kadda ka beri jakuna en taffo kussa ga giddana da derri don ban iya ba en berchi, idan su yi dummi diawa.

Is your friend older than you? I do not know, for I cannot tell how old my friend is. What is the price of an egg in Hausaland? The Hausas do not eat eggs

---

[1]) *kwana* is properly the 24 hours of day and night; the verb *kwana* means 'to pass the night'.

themselves, but if a stranger asks they will bring them
to him. The price of an egg is twenty or thirty cowries.
In the towns they are dearer. When you go far away
from a town they are cheaper. A horse is dearer than
a donkey, but cheaper than a camel. You cannot buy
camels south of Kano because camels are not of any
use there.

Lesson XIII.

200	*dari biu* or *metin*.	2000	*alfin*.
300	*dari uku*.	10,000	*zambar goma*.
400	*arbamia*.	100,000	*zambar dari*.
500	*dari biar*.	1,000,000	*alif alif*, or *dubu*
1000	*dubu, zambar*, or *alif*.		*dari goma*.

The cardinal numbers do not admit of gender; they
follow the nouns or pronouns with which they are
connected. *daia* is combined with the personal pronouns;
thus *daianmu* 'one of us'; *daianku* 'one of you'; *daiansu*
'one of them'.

The *ordinal numbers* are formed by prefixing *na*
masc. or *ta* fem. to the cardinal numbers, except in
the case of the first.

masc.	fem.	
nafari	*tafari*	first.
nabiu	*tabiu*	second.
naüku	*taüku*	third.

nabaia m. *tabaia* f. 'after' is often used for 'second'.
Above ten, cardinal numbers are usually employed instead of ordinals.

The *adverbial numerals* 'once', 'twice' etc. are formed

by prefixing *so* to the cardinal numbers; thus, *sodaia* 'once'; *sobiu* 'twice'; *soüku* 'thrice' etc.

The *distributive numerals* are formed by repeating the cardinal; thus, *ya kilga kurdi biar biar* 'he counted the cowries out by fives', or, *ya bada biu biu ga mutane* 'he gave two to each of the men'.

Fractional numbers. Half is expressed by *shashi* or *rabi* (from *raba* 'to divide'); the other fractions have been obviously borrowed from the Arabic. Those most commonly used are *sulusi* 'a third', *rubuï* 'a quarter', *sudusi* 'a sixth', *subuï* 'a seventh', *sumuni* 'an eighth'. The word *zaka* 'a tenth' is usually applied to the tithe given as alms.

> *kaia* or *kaya* a load. *maikaia* carrier.
> *rude* to deceive. *ya*, O, a title of address.
> *taffi da* (followed by a noun) to take away.

EXERCISE XIII

enna kurdin rakumi nan? rakumina nagari ni, ya zo dagga sokoto, kurdinsa zambar dari da kurdi alfin, ba shina da tsada ba, ya komo dagga so kotoso fudu. sai na baka rubui, en ba ka so ka karba ba, taffi da shi. na sani kwarai kurdinsa ba ka iya ba ka rudeni. ya madugu rabba kurdi nan tsakan masukaia, ka basu dubu dubu. mutum nan ya rudeni so uku ba zan yi chiniki da shi. kadda ka kilga kurdinka shidda shidda amma kilgasu hakka biar biar.

The price of a good camel in the Kano market is from 120,000 to 600,000 cowries; the price of a horse is from 50,000 to 300,000. You can buy a donkey for half the price of a horse, or about a sixth the price of a good camel. What is the price of a slave in Kano? The price of a girl is about 200,000, the price of a boy is 150,000; a man is cheaper than a boy. Men do not care to buy an old man or an old woman. Every day you can see about 500 slaves in the market. In the market of Zaria there are about 200 slaves for sale every day.

LESSON XIV.

The *adjective* usually follows the noun which it qualifies; thus, *mutum nágari* 'a good man'; *rua kaddan* 'a little water'. It is placed before the noun when it is specially desired to emphasise the idea conveyed by the adjective; in this case *n* is placed between it and the noun following; thus, *baban sariki* 'a great king'. There are very few (1) genuine adjectives in Hausa. Many words used as adjectives are either (2) past participles of verbs or (3) are formed by prefixing certain adverbs to nouns.

Adjectives are inflected in order to express gender and number. The masculine gender may end in any vowel, the feminine ends in *a* or in some modification of *a*, such as *ia*, *una* or *unia*. There is no distinction of gender in the plural, the termination of which is usually *ye* or *u*. *nágari* 'good' forms its feminine *tágari*.

masc.	fem.	plur.	
1[1]) *baba*		*mainya*	great.
bakki	*bakka*	*babaku*	black.

---

1) The following is an approximate list of all the simple adjectives.

masc.	fem.	plur.	
dainyi		*dainyoyi*	fresh, raw.
dogo	*dogue*	*dogayi*	tall.
fari	*fara*	*farufaru*	white.
gajiri	*gajira* or *gajiria*	*gajiru*	short.
ja		*jajayi*	red.
kaddan			small, few.
kafo	*kafa*	*kafi*	blind.
karami	*karama*	*karamai* or *kanana*	small, little.
mugu	*mugunia*	*miagu*	bad.
sabo	*sabua*	*sabi*	new.
tsofo	*tsofua*	*tsofi*	old.
wofi			empty, bare, worthless.
2. *achike* or *chikake*	*achika* or *chikaka*	*achiku* or *chikaku*	full.
akunche			untied.
awanke			washed.
dafafe	*dafafa*	*dafafu*	cooked.
konane	*konana*	*konanu*	burnt.
3. *da anfani*			useful.
da hankali			sensible.
da kiyo			good, beautiful.
da rai			alive.
maizini			sharp.
maras hankali			senseless.
maras kumia			shameless.
rashin karifi			weak.

da, when used as above, is equivalent to 'possessed of'; *rashin* 'without' is derived from *rassa* 'to lose'; *maras* is for *ma-rashin*.

maikuturta leper.
dawa guinea-corn.
berkono pepper.
zumua honey.
makafo pl. *makafi* a blind
    person.

kwara grain.
duchi pl. *duatsu* a stone.
nika to grind.
massa a small cake.

EXERCISE XIV.

akoi masukuturta chikkin kano su yi kusa dubu. masu-
gari ba su koresu ba amma su bersu en sayes abubua chikkin kasua. masukuturta ba su so ba su chi kifaye, idan
ka tambaia maikuturta, domi ba ka chi kifi ba, zashi
fada maka, ban sanni·ba, amma mutane duka sun che
ba shi da kiyo ba ga masukuturta. akoi makafi mainya
mainya chikkin kano daiansu sunansa sarikin makafi.
masuchiniki su bada zaka makafi. kadda ka chi dawa
nan sai awankata.

What food do the Hausas eat? Nearly all of them
eat a small red grain which they call *dawa*. The women
grind it with stones, and put water and pepper with it.
Not very many Hausas eat meat, but they like to eat
it when they can get it. Bread is sold in the market
five or six months in each year. They put much pepper
in it too. The Hausas do not like any food without
pepper. They sell cakes which are made with *dawa*,
rice and honey. When they are hungry they will eat
anything which they can get. A white man cannot eat
their food because they put too much pepper in it.

LESSON XV.

An adjective in the singular is very often joined to a substantive in the plural. This is sometimes due to the fact that the substantive is regarded as a collective, but more often it is probably due to carelessness. Adjectives are very often used as substantives, especially when they refer to men or women; thus, *baba* 'great', or 'a great man'.

There is no regular formation in Hausa to express degrees of *comparison*. The following are some of the commonest forms of circumlocution, used in order to express such.

1. Emphasis is expressed by the repetition of the adjective; thus, *kaddan* 'a little', *kaddan kaddan* 'a very little'.

2. The comparative is often expressed by the use of the word *fi* 'to excel'; thus: *abokina ya fini da kiyo* 'my friend is more beautiful than I'. *mineni kana so ya fi wonan* 'what do you want better than this'. *ya fini da wuya* 'this thing is too difficult for me'; *mafi kunchen* 'very narrow' or 'narrower'.

3. The word 'better' is sometimes expressed by *gara;* thus, *gara hakka* 'it is better so'; *gouma* is occasionally used in the same way.

4. 'Better', in the sense of improvement, is expressed by *dama* or *rongomi*; thus, *ka ji dama ya fi jia* 'do you feel better than yesterday?' *na ji rongomi yo* 'I feel better today'.

5. The superlative is usually expressed by *fi* followed
   by *duka* 'all'. *Alla ya fisu duka da girima* 'God
   is the greatest', lit. 'surpasses all in greatness'.
   wonan ya fi duka da noyi 'this is the heaviest'.
   gabba 'before' is sometimes used in the same way,
   shi ni baba gabba ga duka 'he is the greatest',
   lit. 'he is great before all'.

fayi 'to abound' is used in a somewhat similar way;
thus, *makafi sun fayi talauchi* 'blind men are very
poor'.

samu 'to take', 'to find', *chiwo* 'sickness', *da chiwo* 'ill
or to be ill', *tausayi* 'pity, sorrow', *faskare* to be unable
to do anything, usually as an impersonal verb; thus,
ya faskareni 'it is beyond my power'.

EXERCISE XV.

kai yaro ka doka kaian taffi giddana da shi, ba ya
fika nauyi ba (*or* ba ya faskareka ba). aa ya sidi ya
faskareni, amma en kana so zan beri shashi wuri nan
ni komo dagga giddanka massa massa. sanu sanu
abokina na ji tausayi diawa don bawanka ya fada
mani jia kana da chiwo. na godi maka amma na ji
dama yo ina da chiwo jia kaddan kaddan. kai maichiniki ka taffi da kaianka ba zan sayeshi ba don ya fi
tsada duka da na gani chikkin kasua.

The Hausas are stronger than all the other peoples
near to them. If you ask a Hausa whence he gets his
strength, he will tell you that all people who eat guinea-
corn are strong. The Yorubas who eat yams can only
carry half what the Hausas carry. If you take Hausas

as carriers you need only take half as many as if you take others. A white man cannot carry more than half the load that a Hausa will carry.

LESSON XVI.

There are a large number of *Adverbs* in Hausa which are used to denote place, time, manner etc. The following list contains those most commonly used. Several of them are compounds of prepositions and other adverbs. Many of the simple forms are used also as prepositions; cf. Lesson XVII.

Place.

nan here.

chan there.

dagganan whence? or from here.

daggachan thence.

kussa near of nearly.

nesa or *nisa* far away.

tari together.

gabbadai or *gabadai* together.

enna where.

dagga enna whence.

koenna anywhere.

Time.

yanzu now.

yaushi when?

saanda when.

koyanzu now immediately.

koyaushi at any time, always.

kuma again.

hario again.

saanan then.

kaddai or *kadai* once, only, alone.

har or *hal* until.

tunda while, while as yet.

tunyaushi how long?

dafari at first.

da safi in the morning.

da maretchi in the evening.

abbada or *halabbada* for ever.

kulum always.

nan da nan immediately.

Manner.

hakka thus.

hakkanan in this way.

kaka or *kakka* how?	Affirmation or Negation.
tilas by force.	*ai* really.
ko kakka anyhow.	*aje* or *ashe* truly.
kwarai rightly, properly.	*aa* no.
dakir with difficulty.	*i* or *ii* yes.
massa quickly.	*naam* yes.
sanu slowly.	

The preposition *da* 'with' is frequently joined either to an adjective or a noun in order to form an adverb; thus, *dadadi* 'sweetly', *dakarifi* 'powerfully'.

The following adverbs are only used in the expressions here mentioned, *sai* 'quite', *sai lafia* 'quite well'; *lau* is used with *lafia* in order to strengthen it, *lafia lau* 'very well'; *wur* 'very', *ja wur* 'very red'; *fet* 'very', *farifet* 'very white'; *kerrin* 'very', *bakki kerrin* 'very black'.

jima to wait.	*jini* blood.
berichi or *berchi* to sleep.	*gajia* weariness.
tashi to rise.	*ji gajia* to be tired.
tada to raise up.	

EXERCISE.

kai abokina kadda ka taffi ga giddanka amma en mu zamna tari, da safi zamu taffi gabbadai. ka iya-n-gaia mani kakka mutum nan ya mutu? aa ban sani ba kwarai, na komo nan da nan dagga nesa. aje ba ka iya-n-rudeni ba hakka, na sani kwarai ka taffo dagga giddanka koyanzu. kai yaro jima kaddan har na komo gareka. zani zo da maretchi ko gobi da safi. aa ina jin tsoron zamna ni kaddai, ka komo gareni massa massa. hausawa suna da fuska bakka kerrin amma jininsu kaman jini na mutane duka ja wur shi ki. kai maikaia tashi massa

massa kana son berichi hal abbada? idan ba ka tashi
koyanzu zan tadaka tilas. ka bernin berichi hario don
na ji gajia da gaskia, ba na berichi ba jia ko shekaranjia.

Go and tell the carriers to get up immediately, as
I wish to start from here now. Tell them to light a
fire and cook something to eat before they start. If
they do not do so, they will not be able to walk quickly,
but will feel tired, and will want to stop and go to
sleep again. Light the fire anywhere; but do not come
to me again until you have lit it, and have cooked the
food. Go very slowly, or wait here until I come back
to you; when I have untied the camel, I will come
again to you. The boy says that your horse is dead.
It has eaten nothing since the day before yesterday;
it walked yesterday with difficulty. We must leave it
here and start immediately, as we cannot get anything
to eat till we again reach the town from which we
started.

LESSON XVII.

The following are the *Prepositions* most commonly
used:

da to, with.
ga to, for.
na of.
ma to.
dagga from.
tari da together with.
gare or *gari* to, for.

gurubin or *gun* instead of.
biggeri instead of.
wurin in place of.
chikkin in, into.
dagga chikkin in, from within.
tun or *tunda* as far as, until.

4

bisa or *bissa* above, on.

kalkashin or *kalikashin* under.

dagga kalkashin from beneath.

baya or *baya ga* behind.

gabba or *gabba ga* before, in front of.

kussa ga near to.

zakkanin in the midst of.

gum with, in the place of.

maras without, lit. wanting.

bamda apart from, in addition to.

woje or *dagga woje* outside.

sabbada or *sabada* on account of, in exchange for.

sai except, (until).

don because of.

domin because of.

garin for.

akan 'above' (cf. *akan doki* 'on horse back') is perhaps derived from *a kai n* 'on the head of'. *ya zua* lit. 'he goes' is used as a preposition meaning 'towards' or 'to', thus, *ta shudi ya zua birni* 'she went away to the city'.

A large number of the above are substantives which are used as prepositions usually with *n* (a shortened form of *na*) suffixed. As stated before, *gare* is used with the personal pronouns where *ga* would be used with nouns. *ma* is used after certain verbs eg. *fada* 'to speak'; it is also used with the personal pronouns eg. *maka* 'to you', *masu* 'to them'. For use of *garin* cf. *garin zawo* '(he went) for a walk'.

aiki work.

yin aiki to work.

kwarikwassa travelling ants.

ajere in line.

zunzua pl. *zunzaye* bird.

EXERCISE XVII.

ina so ka bani rakuminka, zan baka dokina guru-binsa. aa zan baka alfadari wurin dokinka amma rakumi

ya fi doki da tsada. taffi dagga woje giddana ba zan
yi chiniki ba da ka. en ka hawa dokina na ji tsoro
kadda shi gudu da ka fada akass. mi zaka bani gurubin
sanda nan? zan baka babu bamda wonan. kai maikaya
taffi gabba gareni don en kana taffi baya zaka berichi.
ina so masukaya duka su taffi ajere tunda gari.

There are some ants in the Hausa country which
travel over the land in line; they are very numerous,
no one can count them. Some of them do work and
some are soldiers. The soldiers walk outside the wor-
kers. If they come to a wall, they do not turn back,
but they go up it and then down beyond it. When
men see them coming, they are afraid and run away.
The ants eat everything that they can find which is
living. They do not like anything dead to eat. When
they go away from a house they leave nothing living
behind them. They climb the trees, and eat birds or
monkeys if they can find them.

LESSON XVIII.

The following are the *Conjunctions* most commonly used.

da and.

da ... da both ... and.

amma but.

kua also.

ko either, or, even.

kadda lest.

koda although.

en whether, if, that, in
order that.

don because, in order that.

kaddan or *kadan* if.

hakka or *hakkanan* thus,
likewise.

kamma like as.

kammada like as, according as.

sai only, until.

idan if.

har until.

The use of (the Arabic) *idan* for 'if', is chiefly confined to the neighbourhood of the R. Niger, in Kano *en* is regularly employed.

Of the above, *da*, *don* and *sai* are used both as conjunctions and as prepositions (cf. Lesson XVII). Thus we may say *don wonan na bashi kurdi don shi ya yi chiniki da shi* 'for this reason I gave him money in order that he might trade with it'; *sai ka tsofi* '(wait) till you grow old', B. 115; *tsofua sai jiwoji* 'an old woman (has) nothing but veins', C. 19.

mutu 'to die' is used in several different senses; thus, *mutum ya mutu* 'the man is dead', *wata* [1]) *ya mutu* 'the month is ended', *hainya ta mutu* 'the way is closed', *tukunia ta mutu* 'the pitcher is broken'.

yi 'to make' or 'to do' is used idiomatically; thus, *wonan ya yi wonchan* 'this is equal to that'; *wonan ya yi kaman wonchan* 'this is the same as that'; *ya yi* 'it does', i. e. 'it is satisfactory'.

yi karia lit. 'to make a lie' is used for 'to miss'; thus, *bindiga ya yi karia* 'the gun missed fire'. *zuchia* 'heart' is used idiomatically; thus, *ya che chikkin zuchia* 'he thought', lit. 'he said in his heart'.

abduga cotton or cotton plant.	*saka* to weave.
zarre thread.	*kadi* to spin.
abawa thick cotton yarn.	*kada* spindle.
rimi silk-cotton tree.	*rinni* or *rini* to dye.
marina dye-pit.	*baba* indigo.
tufa or *tufua* pl. *tufafi* a shirt.	*riga* pl. *riguna* a robe, gown.

---

1) *wata* and *hainya* are sometimes regarded as masc. sometimes as fem. thus we may also say *wata ta mutu*, *hainya ya mutu*. The gender of many other words is thus variable.

EXERCISE XVIII.

akoi marinai mainya mainya chikkin kano. mutane masurini su kawo tufafinsu su sasu chikkin marinai su bersu kwana uku ko wotakila kwana bokkoi, su sa baba diawa chikkin marinai tari da tufafi, saanda tufafi arinasu masurini su dokasu dagga marinai, su sayesu ga masu-chiniki chikkin kasua. riga maikiyo kurdinsa zambar ar-baïn ko hamsin, kadan riga aberta chikkin marina har wata daia ya mutu babu anfaninta. kai abokina riga wonda na saida dagga gareka ba ta yi ba don ba asa-kata ba da kiyo.

The thread which the Hausa people spin is not made from the silk-cotton tree, but from the cotton plant. You cannot spin that which is made from the silk-cotton tree on a spindle, because it is not strong. The men and women in Kano spin the cotton in their houses or outside in the road or market place, and when it is spun they weave it and make robes and shirts with it. Then they carry them to the owners of the dye-pits who dye them with indigo. One third or perhaps half the people in Kano either spin or weave cotton. Many of the robes which they make are beautiful, the traders buy them in the markets and carry them to distant places in order to sell them.

LESSON XIX.

The *Interjections* in ordinary use are, *kai*, *ya*, *wai*. The first, which is perhaps a strengthened form of *ka* 'thou', is used in calling a person in order to attract his attention as *kai yaro* 'ho boy!' *ya* is most commonly met with in the expression borrowed from the Arabic *ya sidi* 'Sir', or 'O Sir'. *wai* 'alas'! is used by itself, cf. F. 159. *wai* is also sometimes used as an expression of doubt or incredulity. *hubba* is used to express astonishment or indignation.

The following are some of the commonest forms of salutation employed.

sanu or *sanu sanu* hail!
sanu da rana good morning!
sanu da derri good night!
sanu da maretchi good evening!
kana lafia, or *sai lafia*, or *lafia* how do you do!
lafia lau good health to you!
agaisheka or *agaisheku* hail!
sai gobi good bye till tomorrow!
sai wota rana farewell till another day!
sai anjima good bye for the present (i. e. I am just
    coming back, or come back quickly!)

The word *sanu* is sometimes repeated a dozen or more times in order to add emphasis to the greeting. Its meaning often varies according to the word which follows it. Thus, *sanu da aiki* 'may you be happy over your work'. *sanu da gajia* lit. 'greetings to your weariness' i. e. 'I hope you are not overtired'. If a man meets you when it is raining he will say *sanu da rua* i. e. 'welcome to you amidst the rain'.' *sanu* is sometimes joined on to the personal pronouns; thus, *sanuku* 'hail to you!'

The word *to* is used as a sort of interjection, meaning

'well', 'so', or 'indeed'. If a native does not quite understand what is said he will frequently reply *to*. If a Hausa wishes to be thought learned he will usually begin with the Arabic form of salutation, *salam alaik* 'peace be upon thee!' to which the person saluted is expected to reply *alaikum salam* 'upon you be peace'.

EXERCISE XIX.

sanu de rana sariki? sanu da rana aboki, sanu sanu kana lafia? lafia lau sariki na godi allah. waneni kai enna ka fito? ni bako ni na taffo nan dagga nesa en gaisheka. mi kana so da ni? ina son kana bernin yi chiniki chikkin kasua. to, taffi giddanka sai jibi. zan taffi koyanzu sariki zan aiki kua kaya abin gaisua gareka, baya nan zan komo, sanu sanu sai anjima.

When two men meet each other., although they are strangers and have not seen each other before, they stop to salute. Sometimes they will salute each other ten or twelve times, before they go on again. Before doing business with a merchant it is necessary to salute him, although you know that after saluting you in return, he will begin to tell lies and try to cheat you.

ADDITIONAL GRAMMATICAL NOTES.

LESSON XX.

Substantives.

The *genitive case* is very frequently expressed by a circumlocution instead of by means of a preposition.;

thus, instead of saying *surdin doki* 'the saddle of the horse', it would be more usual to say *doki] surdinsa* 'the horse its saddle', cf. A 60 *sheggi wanda babu uba nasa shi ni uwa tasa ta bi wanda ta fandari*, lit. 'a bastard who there is no father to him he his mother follows that which is crooked'. i. e. 'a bastard who had no father and whose mother followed a crooked path'. The construction of this line, which affords a good illustration of Hausa writing, closely resembles that of Arabic.

Abstract substantives usually end either in *chi* or *ta*. e. g. *ragonchi* 'idleness', from *rago* 'idle'; *diyauchi* 'freedom', from *dia* 'free'; *chiwuta* 'sickness', from *chiwo* 'ill'; *mugunta* 'wickedness', from *mugu* 'bad'. In several cases forms with both suffixes are found; thus, *kuturchi* or *kuturta* 'leprosy', from *kuturu* 'to be leprous'. *bauchi*, *bawanchi* or *bauta* 'slavery', from *bawa* 'a slave'.

There are however many words ending both in *chi* and *ta* which do not represent abstract ideas e. g. *machi* 'woman', *sarota* 'kingdom'.

The suffix *chi* sometimes denotes the office or work of a person or thing, e. g. *turanchi* 'that which belongs to the Arabs', 'the Arab language'; *taka* is used as a suffix in a somewhat similar sense, e. g. *bakontaka* 'strangeness', from *bako* 'a stranger', *yi bakontaka* 'to feel as a stranger'; *barantaka* 'service', from *bara* 'a servant'; *diantaka* 'freedom' is used in the same way as *diyauchi*.

ba is used as a prefix to denote origin or ancestry; thus, *ba-haushe* 'a Hausa native', *ba-laraba* 'an Arab' (pl. *larabawa*), *ba-ture* 'an Arab', an expression applied to any white man. *dan* 'son of' is frequently used in the sense of 'native of'; thus, *dan zaria* 'a native' or 'inhabitant of Zaria'. It is also used as a diminutive, e. g. *dan kasua* 'a little market', or to express general relation of any kind, e. g. *dan daki* 'servant', lit. 'son of the room', *dan yaki* 'soldier'.

The prefix *mai* which is used to denote the noun-agent cf. p. 20, is probably a contracted form of *ma-yi* i. e. 'the one who does'. It may often be rendered 'the man of', e. g. *maigaskia* 'the man of truth'.

The prefix *ma* is sometimes used together with the suffix *chi* to denote the agent; thus, *mafauchi* 'butcher' from *fawa* 'to slaughter'; *maaikachi* 'workman' from *aiki* 'to work'.

The Verb.

In the Semitic languages proper the verbal stem undergoes a series of changes, by the addition of various prefixes, by doubling one of the existing consonants, or by modification of the vowel sounds. In this way some fifteen voices or changes of meaning somewhat resembling voices are obtained. In the Berber language, to which Hausa is probably allied, there are ten such voices, though the changes in the verbal stem do not bear any close resemblance to those of Arabic. In Hausa there appear to be traces of four or five such, though with the exception of the ordinary passive formation, it is doubtful whether it is possible to connect them with any uniform changes of meaning. The suffixes used are *shi*, *da*, *es*, *esda* or *asda*, *chi*. Very few verbs

possess more than two or, at the most, three of these
additional forms.

The following are examples of such changes:

ba 'to give'; *bashi* and *bayes* 'to give up', 'to deliver
up to'; *bada*, usually joined with some other word, e. g.
bada girima 'to honour', *bada gaskia* 'to acquit', *bada
laifa* 'to condemn'; used with *hainya* 'road' it means
'to lead'. *hainya ya badamu* 'the road led us to'; *bayesda*
'to restore'.

tara 'to collect', 'to bring together'; *taras* or *tarda* 'to
overtake', 'to come up with', e. g. *na tardashi* 'I overtook
him'; *tarshi* 'to meet or to help', cf. D. 48, *ka tar-
shimu ji dadi* 'help us to feel happy'; *tari* 'to meet' or
'to go to meet', (cf. also the preposition *tari* or *tari da*
'together with').

chi 'to eat'; *chida* or *chishi* 'to feed on' or 'to give to
eat'.

zuba, *zubas* or *zubasda* 'to pour'; *zubda* 'to upset'
(water).

bata, *bachi*, *batas*, *batasda* 'to spoil' or 'to destroy'; *batasda* is used with *hainya*; thus, *na batasda hainya* 'I lost
my way'.

kwana or *kwanchi* 'to sleep'; *kwanta* 'to spend the
night'.

manta or *manchi* 'to forget'.

berchi or *berichi* 'to sleep' may perhaps be a modification of *ber* or *beri* 'to leave'.

In addition to the passive formation given in Lesson
IV the suffix *u* is frequently used to denote a passive,
or at least an intransitive sense; thus, *bude* 'to open',

budu 'to be open' or 'to be opened'. *nade* 'to roll up', *nadu* 'to be rolled up', or 'to roll oneself up'. *tara* 'to collect', *taru* 'to assemble'. The ordinary form of the Hausa verb ends either in *a*, *e*, *i*, *o*, or *u*.

It seems impossible to assign any distinct meanings to the first three terminations; they are found also in Fulah and Nupé. Many verbs seem to be used indifferently with each in turn.

The termination *o* suggests movement towards the speaker or something done for the benefit of the speaker; thus, *taffi* 'to go', *taffo* 'to come'; *gusa* 'to move a little back', guso 'to move a little forward'; wanko 'wash it and bring it back'! Sometimes however it is difficult to trace any such meaning; thus, *koiya* 'to teach', *koiyo* 'to learn'. In some cases *o* is the only suffix employed; thus, *yawo* 'to go for a walk'.

The terminations *ia*, *ua*, *uwa* usually give to the verb a participial meaning. They are also frequently used as the present indicative of the verb; thus, *taffia* 'going', *zakua* 'coming', *taffowa* 'coming'. They are also found as substantival forms; thus, *taffia* 'a journey', *mutua* 'dying' or 'death'.

The form *zani* 'I will' is often shortened into *ni* e. g. *ina tamaha ni sameshi* 'I think that I shall find him'.

The particle *kan* (which is perhaps a defective verb, of which no other form remains) gives to the verb with which it is used a frequentative meaning; thus, *ni kan taffi* 'I was in the habit of going'. It also suggests permission to do a thing; thus, *ka kan taffi* 'thou mayest go'.

The following table exhibits the various modifications of the pronouns in the different tenses.

	Present.		Aorist or Indefinite.		Perfect.	Future.	Subjunctive or Concessive.
	Simple.	Emphatic.	Simple.	Emphatic.			
Sing. 1.	ina	ni ki	na	ni na	ni na, or nika	zani or ni	ni kan
2.	kana	ka ki	ka	kai ka	kaka	zaka	ka kan
	kina	ki ki	ki	ki ki	kika	zaki	ki kan
3.	shina	shi ki	ya	shi ya	shika	zashi	shi kan
	tana	ta ki	ta	ita ta	taka	zata	ta kan
Plural 1.	muna	mu ki	mu	mu mu	muka	zamu	mu kan
2.	kuna	ku ki	ku	ku ku	kuka	zaku	ku kan
3.	suna	su ki	su	su su	suka	zasu	su kan

In the Perfect tense *n* is often inserted before the final '*ka*'; this is especially the case in the plural, thus we get *munka, kunka, sunka*.

The Aorist forms are very frequently used where a future sense is intended; in the passive this use of the Aorist for the future is the rule rather than the exception.

This use of the Aorist for the future is parallel to the Arabic use of the Perfect for the purpose of expressing the future in certain classes of events, e. g. to express an act, the occurrence of which is so certain that it may be described as having already taken place; in promises, bargains, oaths and asseverations [1]).

In Hausa the same form is frequently employed as substantive and verb; thus, *aiki* 'work' or 'to work'. The phenomenon is one well known to students of language; compare the widely accepted theory of Dietrich that the 3rd Pers. forms of the Semitic Imperfect were originally substantival. Max Müller [2]) points out that the terminations of the Turkish Imperfect, as *severdi-m* 'I loved', are identical with the suffix pronouns used after nouns, as *baba-m* 'my father', and infers that 'what remains after their removal must have been originally a substantive'.

The force of verbs is frequently intensified by the reduplication of the first syllable or by the actual repetition of the word; thus, *tsaga* 'to tear', *tsatsaga* 'to tear to pieces'; *chika* 'to fill', *chichika* 'to fill quite full'; *sanni* or *sani* 'to know', *sansanchi* 'to understand well'; for instances of the repetition of the word cf. *buga buga* 'to strike repeatedly', *gushe gushe* 'to gush out abundantly'.

Nouns and adverbs are reduplicated in a similar way; thus, *safi* 'morning', *sasafi* 'very early in the morning', *massa* 'quickly', *massa massa* 'very quickly'.

Interchange of Letters. The following letters are sometimes interchanged, *p* and *f*. cf. *pansa* or *fansa* 'a

---

1) Cf. Wright's Arabic Grammar. Vol. II, 1e and f.
2) Science of Language. Vol. I. pp. 356 seqq.

reward'. In writing there is no Hausa letter to represent *p*, *f* being used instead.

f and *h*. cf. *huska* for *fuska* 'face', A 67; *hutawa* for
futawa 'rest', B 62; *fuja* for *huja* 'affair'.

l and *r*. *kilga* and *kirga* 'to count', *biar* and *bial*
'five', *yar gidda* for *yan gidda* 'son of the house'.

l and *n*. *kamal* for *kaman* 'like', A 13.

f and *w*. *fuche* for *wuche* 'to pass away'.

t and *h*. *halita* and *talita* 'a created being'.

n is changed to *m* before *b*; thus, an *em bika* (not
en bika) 'shall I follow you'? [1])

In rapid conversation the final vowel sound of the
Personal Pronouns is frequently suppressed. This is
especially the case in Kano. Thus, *taffi gareshi* or *taffi
garesa* 'go to him' is pronounced *taffi garuss*; *fada
masa* 'say to him' is pronounced *fada muss*.

LESSON XXI.

COMMON OR IDIOMATIC EXPRESSIONS.

kana lafia or *sanu sanu* how do you do?
sai lafia na godi allah quite well, I thank God.
godia, *na yi godia*, or *na godi* thank you.
enna (or *ina*) *labari* what is the news?
ban ji ba komi I have heard nothing.
kana yin magana hausa do you speak Hausa?
aa amma ina son ka koya mani magana hausa no, but
    I wish you would teach me Hausa.

---

1) for similar change in Arabic cf. *min baiti* 'from the house' pronounced *mim baiti*.

mi ka che what did you say?

kadda ka yi magana da sauri do not speak fast.

tambayeni woni magana da ni yi kokari en amsa maka ask me anything and I will try to answer you.

ban ji ba I do not understand.

mineni dabamchi (or *babamchi*) *wonan da wonchan* what is the difference between this and that?

ban sani ba kwarai I do not know at all.

duka daia ni or *swa swa* it is all the same.

woni lokachi ni what time is it?

lokachin tashi ni it is time to get up.

kadda ka deddi hakka do not delay thus.

kaka deddiwanka da zaka kari aikinka how long will you be before you finish your work?

ya kari it is finished.

ya issa it is enough.

ya issheni or *ya iskeni* it is enough for me.

gáfera excuse me, or I beg your pardon.

ya yi arziki it is fortunate.

rufe kofa shut the door.

bude kofa open the door.

rana ta yi or *ya yi rana* it is daylight.

rana tana da zafi it is hot.

shekkarunka nawa or *shekkara nawa kana da rai* or *shekkara nawa tun haifuanka* how old are you?

sai ambideka wait till you are sent for.

ba shi kai hakkanan ba the price is too much.

ba su san abin da zasu yi ba they know not what to do.

na ji dama kaddan kaddan I feel a little better.

kana ji massassara have you got fever?

na yi murna na isheka (or *na sameka*, or *na gamu*

da kai) da hainya I am glad that I met you on the
road.

taffi sanu sanu go slowly.

en mu taffi yawo (or *garin yawo*) let us go for a walk.

giddanga ta fayi kankanta this house is too small.

itachi nan ya fayi tsawo this tree is very tall.

*itatua nan suna da enua dayawa en mu zamna kalkas-
hinsu* these trees are very shady, let us sit down under them.

ka iya yi karatu rubutunga can you read this writing?

ban karba ba I do not believe it, lit. I do not receive.

kana yi magana kaman rua you speak fluently, lit. you
speak like water.

DAYS OF THE WEEK.

rana lahadi	Sunday.
„	*latini*	Monday.
„	*talata*	Tuesday.
„	*laraba*	Wednesday.
„	*alhamis*	Thursday.
„	*aljimua*	Friday.
„	*assubat*	Saturday.

HOURS OF THE DAY APPROXIMATELY.

jijifi twilight just before the dawn.

azuba dawn.

hanchi two hours after dawn i. e. about 8 a. m.

wollata about 10 a. m.

rana tsaka midday.

zowall about 2 p. m.
azuhur „ 4 p. m.
laasar „ 6 p. m.
maguriba late in the evening.
lisha very late in the evening.
(Nearly all the above are modifications or corruptions of the Arabic).

EXPRESSIONS USED IN BUYING AND SELLING.

enna rongomi? what are you going to allow me? (literally 'where is the deduction', this is the usual phrase used in asking for the discount on a large ready money transaction.)

enna gara? how much are you going to give me into the bargain? (when a man buys nuts or anything else in a small way, he gets his fifty or a hundred cowries worth and so many extra thrown in for luck; this is called the *gara* or addition).

Buyer. *rakumi nan na sayerua* is this camel for sale?

Seller. *i* yes.

Buyer. *ba shi suna* name its price. lit. give it a name.

Seller. *zambar metin ou hamsin* two hundred and fifty thousand cowries. (*ou* is the Arabic „ 'and').

Seller. *hubba munna ya fi na baka dari da hamsin* indeed! that is too much for me, I will give you one hundred and fifty thousand.

Buyer. *alberka* no thank you. (*alberka* [1]) is used in salutations for 'thank you', but in the language of the market it is equivalent to 'no thank you').

---

1) Compare use of *merci* in French.

5

ladda woji, *ladda chikki*. If a man sells anything in the market or through a broker *ladda woji* (lit. 'reward without'), he receives the whole of the money paid, and the buyer pays the market fee or the broker's commission; if however the transaction is concluded *ladda chikki* (lit. 'reward within'), the reverse obtains. The usual *ladda*, i. e. discount, is five per cent on the whole amount involved.

chi riba 'to make profit' usually implies that the seller has been cheated by the transaction.

HAUSA READINGS.

INTRODUCTORY NOTE.

In the specimens of Hausa writing, which are here given, the student will notice that the system of representing the Hausa sounds by Arabic letters is by no means uniform. Different scribes employ different systems of transcription, and the same writer will sometimes transcribe a word differently in two consecutive lines. This is especially the case in regard to the use of the letters ا ي و ع. Were it not the case that the Arabic alphabet is taught in the native schools and is understood by many thousands of the Hausas, it would not be worth while troubling the student with the Arabic alphabet at all. But as it is essential that he should be in a position to understand letters or other documents, which may come into his hands in the country, I have here given several different specimens of Hausa transcribed in the Arabic alphabet. The difficulty suggested by the lack of any uniform system of transcription is greater in theory than in practice. The Hausa sounds are more or less accurately represented by whatever system is adopted and, with the context to act as an additional guide, the meaning is very seldom obscured.

The following rules will be found generally speaking
to hold good.

Verbs, which end with with the sound of the Italian
i, are written with ﺱ as their concluding letter; thus,
دَرْمِی *darmi* 'to bind', D 13.

Substantives ending with this sound, unless the emphasis
lies on the last syllable, are not written with a final ﺱ;
thus, بَکِ *baki* 'mouth', D 11.

Verbs, which end with the sound of the Italian *a*, do
not as a rule take a final ﺍ, whereas substantives ending
with the same sound very frequently do; thus, مَیْدَ *maida*
'to change', D 7. but کَذَا *kaẓa* 'chicken', D 11. As
however the same forms are frequently employed both
as substantives and as verbs it is clear that these rules
must be constantly broken.

Many words, when they stand at the end of a line
in a song, have an additional ﺍ or ﺱ as a final letter,
which they would not otherwise take. Words ending
with the sound *o* occasionally take a final ﺍ; thus, تَفُّوﺍ
taffo 'to come', A. 8. The sound *o* may be represented
by ـُ, ـُو, ـَو, or ـَوﺍ; the sound *u* by ـُ, or ـُو.

Jezm (cf. p. 9) is comparatively seldom inserted over
the letters ﺱوﺍ.

The only sign of punctuation used by the Hausas is
∴, which corresponds to a full stop or semicolon in
English. There is no mark of interrogation used.

I.

Bismi allaḥi errahmani errahimi ṣalla
allaḥu ala saydina muhammadin wa áliḥi wa ṣahbiḥi
wa salaman tasliman

haẓ alkitab alrata limansub

Bismi allaḥi allaḥ fárawa na ḳaratu	suna ni na allaḥ dakanan fára aiki
Ya allaḥ rabbi ka bamu gamu katerta	muna ẓikiri muna addua muna ṣallati
Ya allaḥ ya khaliḳu ya arziḳi bai	maabudu ya rabbana sarki sarota
Ya allaḥ ka shiriamu mu yi aiki ṣawaba	kadda mu kurkura mu yi abinda ba shi kama ba
Ẓamu fa haddichi nị akan majia kalami	ba wonan da kan jishi ba shi kalkadi ba
To matamu almajiri aku- maida ḥimma	kuna ẓikri kuna addua kuna ṣallati
Akuyi nesa ku ber kai da kawowa na karia	ku berta radda ku ber hasada da ananminchi
Ku ji choro akoi rangamu mu da mu da allaḥ	rana na ḳomi ka ki chiki sai ta budi
Enna boiya enna jachiki enna fasada	wata rana akoi damasa ya ka che ba yi ba
Atuba haḳíḳa aboki aber na karia	aber rikichi aber sha gia da bam da buẓa
Ayi tuba ga allaḥ aber tuba maẓoro	shi ki tuba kaẓa ta tana baki bai sako ba.
Maituba maẓoro ba shi ashi kowani ba	sai ẓunubi sai sanduna da su da sarka

Akandarmishi baia baia
ajashi da birkido
Ajashi anadakka hal ta yin
doro aẓába
Shina kuka shina shashasha
ki achiki
Kuma akankaishi kan rataia
ga rinu aẓába
Shi ki nan fa daimu babu
fita dadai ba
Maituba ba shi komo ga
aiki nai na ṣabo
Ayi tuba ga allaḥ aboki
aber na karia
Ayi tuba haḳíḳa aber rikichi
na banẓa
Maiṣuabo iẓan ya ki tuba
ya yi khasára
Ku bi allaḥ ku ber bi läinu
da shi da nafsi

wuta da wuta ta ki wanyi
duka babu kawichi
chikin machichi chikin ga-
mata chikin maṣiba
aẓába ana takura ana dan-
dakasa kamal kilago
shina tsua shina takura
kamal kutara
ba mutua bale shidoshi shi
je shi futa
kun ji fa mun fadi yanda
ka nemasa ba khila fa
aber koiya na shaitan da
ẓashi giddan aẓába
idan haka yi góbi anadubu
nadama
ya rubushi ya kora kansa
chikin aẓába
kuna aẓumi da ṣalla kuna
zaka da haji

In the name of God, the Compassionate, the Merciful,
may God bless our lord Mohammed and his
relations and his friends, and peace be (upon them).

This is written for the instruction of my relations.

In the name of God, God is the beginning of my writing, His name is God, from Him is the beginning
of work.

O God, my Lord, grant us prosperity, we utter invocations, we offer supplications and prayers.

O God, creator and sustainer of thy servants, O my
Lord who art worshipped and rulest over the kingdom.

O God, prepare us that we may work successfully, let
us not fail or do that which is unfitting.

We will speak out, if there is ayone to listen to our
words; that which you hear cast not away.

Ye too O women, my disciples, do you show diligence;
invoke the name of God and offer supplications and
prayers.

Put far away and leave off false dealing, leave off
whispering, leave off jealousy and tale-bearing.

Be afraid, there is a day of meeting between us and
God; on that day whatever your are within shall be
revealed.

Wherever there is any secret, any secret thieving, any
envying, on that day there shall be confusion, he
will say that he did it not.

My friend, repent truly and leave off falsehood, leave
off deceit, leave off drinking gia and bam and buza.

Repent to God, leave off repenting like a wild cat; it
repents with the fowl in its mouth, it puts it not
down.

He who repents like a wild cat shall indeed have nothing but evil, stripes and chains.

He shall be bound with his hands behind, he shall be
dragged backwards and forwards, the fire shall include everything, there shall be no end to it.

He shall be dragged and beaten till the pain causes a
swelling on the back; in the fire is squeezing, faint-
ness and great pain.

He cries, he gasps for breath, pain bows him down,

it strikes him frequently (as though he were) a skin (that is beaten).

Again he is taken and tied to a painful stake, he cries out, he falls down like the beam (for pumping water).

There is indeed for ever no release at all; much less will death take him away, so that he should go to rest.

He who repents, returns not to his work again; do you listen, we say that there will be no giving of bribes then, though you may seek for it.

My friend, you must repent to God, you must leave off falsehood, leave off the teaching of Satan, which tends to the house of pain.

Repent truly, leave off vain deceit; if this be done, on the resurrection day your repentance will be seen.

The evil doer, if he refuses to repent, will suffer misfortune; he loses (all), he hurries himself to (the place of) pain.

Follow God, cease following the wicked man, leave both him and his desires; keep the fast, and pray, and go on the pilgrimage.

[For notes on above passage cf. 'Specimens of Hausa Literature' pp. 44—46.]

II.

The following is revised translation of the Lord's Prayer made by a Hausa mallam from the Arabic.

أَبَـامُ وَنْدَ كِى ثِكِنْ سَمَا سُونَنْكَ يَثَّرْكَكَ سَرَوتَنْكَ تَـذَكَ ··

أَبِنْدَ كَكِى سُو يَكَشِى تَمْكَر ثِكِنْ سَمَا حَكَنَنْ أَبِسَا دُونِيَا ··

أَبِنْثِى دَيَعِشِيمْ كَبَامُ يُو ·· كَغَاٍرْتَ مُنَ ذُنْبَيِمْ كَمَدَ مُو كُمَا

مُنَغَافِرْتَ غَمَاسِينْ دُنْبَى غَرِيمْ ·· كَدَ كَشِغَسْدَمُ أَتِكِينْ جَرَبَا
أَمَا كَيْرَسْدَمُ دَغَ شِيتَانْ ··

ubamu wanda ki chikkin sama. sunanka ya charkaka
sarotanka ta zaka. abinda ka ki so ya kasshi tamkar
chikkin sama hakanan abissa dunia. abinchi da ya ishemu
ka bamu yo. ka gaferta muna zunubaimu kamada mu
kuma muna gaferta ga masuyin zunubai garemu. kadda
ka shigasdamu achikkin jaraba amma ka chirasdamu dagga
shaitan.

NOTES AND ANALYSIS.

أَبَامُ *ubamu* 'our Father' *mu* I P. Pl. inseparable Possessive Pronoun cf. p. 17.

وَنْدَكِى *wanda ki* 'who art' *ki* substantive verb cf. p. 20.
A fuller form, frequently used, would be وَنْدَكَكِى *wanda ka ki.*

ثِكِينْ سَمَا *chikkin sama* 'in heaven', *sama* is a borrowed Arabic word denoting 'heaven' or 'firma-
ment'. Either *sama* or سَمَانِى *samania* can be used as
the plural; cf. Gr. τοῖς οὐρανοῖς.

سُونَنْگ *sunanka* 'thy name' *nka* I. P. Sing. inseparable
Possessive pronoun cf. p. 17.

يَثَرْكَكَ *ya charkaka* 'it is sanctified' or 'may it be sanctified', *charkaka* is used both in an active and passive
sense.

سَرَوتَنْكَ *sarotanka* 'thy kingdom'. Abstract substantives
very frequently end in *ta*, cf. p. 56.

تَذَكَ *ta zaka* 'it comes' or 'let it come'; *ta* 3 P. F. Personal pronoun agreeing with *sarota*; *zaka* a defective verb 'to come'.

أَبِنْدَ كَكِى سُو *abinda ka ki so* lit. 'the thing that thou wishest', for use of *abinda* cf. p. 25.

يَكَشِى *ya kasshi* 'it is' or 'let it be; 'kasshi* 'to be' or ,to exist' is seldom used in colloquial, but is common in written Hausa.

تَمْكَرْثِكِنْ سَمَا *tamkar chikkin sama* 'as in heaven'; in addition to *tamkar* the forms *tamka* and *tamkan* are found.

حَكَنَنْ أَبِسَا دُونِيَا *hakanan abissa dunia* 'so on earth' The forms *bissa* and *abissa* are used indifferently, cf. *chikkin* ثِكِنْ and *achikkin* آثِكِنْ.

أَبِنْثِى دَيَعِشِيمْ كَبَامْ يُو *abinchi da ya isshemu ka bamu yo* 'food that suffices us give us today'. *abinchi* lit. 'a thing to eat', cf. *abinsha* 'drink'. *da* relative pronoun, for other uses cf. p. 24.

كَغَافِرْتَ مُنَ ذُنُبَيِمْ *ka gaferta muna zunubaimu* 'forgive us our sins'; *zunubai* a borrowed Arabic word, in Hausa it is sometimes written ذُنُفَى *zunufai*; *gaferta* cf. common use of *gáfera* in the sense of 'excuse me' or 'I beg your pardon'.

كَمَدَ مُو كُمَا مُنَغَافِرْتَ *kamada mu kuma muna gaferta* 'like as we also forgive'; *kamada* a lengthened form of *kama* 'as' cf. *tamka* and *tamkanda* or *tankanda*.

غَمَاسُيِن زُنُبَى غَرِيمُ *ga masuyin ẓunubai garemu* 'to those who do evil to us' *masuyin* from *yi* 'to do' and *mai*, plural *masu*, which can be prefixed to any verb in order to denote the noun agent, cf. pp. 20; 50, for use of *gare* cf. p. 18.

كَذ كَشِغَسْدَمُ *kadda ka shiggasdamu* 'cause us not to enter, *kadda* a particle expressing prohibition. *shiggasda* a causative form of *shigga* 'to enter', cf. *fita* and *fitasda*.

أَثِكِنْ جَرَبَا *achikkin jaraba* 'into temptation' *jaraba* 'to tempt' or 'to test' cf. II form of Arabic جرب; for use of, cf. A. 65.

أَمَا كَثِرَسْدَمُ دَغَّ شَيْتَانْ *amma chirasdamu ka dagga shaitan* 'but deliver us from the evil one'. *chirasda* 'to take away from' or 'to deliver', cf. *chira* 'to lift up' or 'to arise'.

III.

The capture of Khartum and the death of General Gordon. Description by Hausa native in the Mahdi's camp.

رَاَنْ دَذَاكَمَش اَنْكَي يِكَ تُنّدَ سَابِ حَلْمَرِين بَابُو زَمَنَ ..
مُتَنِنْ بَاش اَنْكَكَش اَنْكَكَش مُتَنِنْ مَحّدِ دَيَو حَلْدِر حَلْاَرَبَ
مُتَنِنْ بَاش سُنْكَبَرِى وَنِ وُرِ سُنْكَدُو وُرِن مَحّدِ سُنْكَثِى
مُنْغَجِى بَابُو بُتَاءَ يُو كُثِيمُ كَدَنْ كُنْتَبِى غِدَ دَدِر بَاش
يَغُدُو .. مَحّدِ يَثِى تُو حَكَ ذَمِيِى مُسَمِيِش مَحّدِ يَبَس

دُكَىَ يَثِى كُتَىِى اِنْ كُسُو كُزُونَ ثِكِنْ سَنْسَىِ اِنْ بَا كُسُو

بَا كُتَىِى غَرِنْكَ .. سُنْگَىِى مُرْنَ يَكَوُ شَنُو اَيِنْكَ دَرْكِمْ

اَنْكَيِنْكَ يَكَوُ كُوردْ دَيَوَ يَبَا مَاسْبَاْدَ يَثِى تُو وَنِن بَا نِيسُو

شِكُونَ سَى مُنْثِش دَعِكِنْ اَلَه .. سَعَنْنَف اَنْكَتَمِش دَاَزْبَ يَكَوُ

مُتَنِ سُنْكَ تَمِى غَبَزْ غَحَرْتُمْ اَنْكَتَمِى غَارِيَوَ مَحَدِ شِنَ

دَعَنَنْ كُدُسْ .. مَحَدِ يَتَنِش اَنْكَيِى بُوسَ دُكَ سُنْتَمِى ذَوَ

حَرْتُمْ مُتَنِ حَرْتُمْ سُنْكَ تَشِى اَنْكَغَمْ اَنْبَدَ وَنِنْ دَوَدَنْ سُنْ

بُغُو بِنْدِغَ حَلْدِرِ سُنْبَدَ بَا سَايَوَ سُشِغَ بَا .. اَنْبَدَ حَرْ غَرِ

يَوِىِى دَجِجِبِ مَحَدِ يَشِغَ غَرِ مُتَنِنْ بَاش دَسُنْگَجِى حَكَنَنْ

رُثِمِنْسُ يَفِدِى .. كَدَنْ مُتَنِ مَحَدِ سُنْسُوكِى مُتُمْ سُنْمِسْدَ

بِنْدِغَ .. مُتُمْ كَمَنْ عِشْرِنْ سُنْكَمَ .. بَاش يَثِى بَا ذَاش

غُدْ بَا حَرْ اَنْكَكَمَش .. اَنْبَغَش دَبِنْدِغَ اَنْكَسِرِيش دَتَكُوبِ ..

مَحَدِ يَثِى اَكَوُ كِمِنْسَ اَنْسَرِيش اَنْدَوكَ نَمَنْسَ اَنْجِيْمَش

ثِكِنْ رَوَ .. كِمِنْسَ اَنْكَوُ وُرِنْ مَحَدِ .. مَحَدِ يَثِى رُىِى

عِلَدَنْ يَثِى كُنْيِى مُوغْنْ اَبُ دُومِ كَكَشِيش يَىِى دُش يَتَشِى

يَكُومُو سَنْسَسِ دَمَرِينْ ..

rana da zaakamashi ankayi yaki tunda safi hal maretchi babu zamna. mutanen basha ankakashi mutanen
mahdi diawa hal derri hal azuba. mutanen basha sunka
beri woni wuri sunka zo wurin mahdi sunka che mun
gaji babu futawa yo ku chimu [1]) kaddan kun taffi gidda
da derri basha ya gudu [2]). mahdi ya che to haka zamu
yi mu sameshi mahdi ya basu dukia ya che ku taffi en

ku so ku zona chikkin sansanni en ba ku so ba ku
taffi garinku. sun kai murna ya kawo shanu ayenka da
rakumi ankayenka ya kawo kurdi diawa ya ba masu-
fada ya che to wanan ba ni so shi kwana sai mun.
chishi da ikon allah. saanan fa ankatashi da azuba ya
kawo mutane sunka taffi gabbaz ga khartum ankataffi
ga ariawa mahdi shina dagganan kuddus. mahdi ya
tashi ankayi busa duka sun taffia zua khartum mutane
khartum sunka tashi ankagamu anafada wanan da wanan [3]) sun bugu bindiga [4]) hal derri sun fada ba su iyawa
ba su shigga ba. anafada har gari ya wayi [5]) da jijifi [6])
mahdi ya shigga gari mutanen basha da sunka ji hakanan zuchiansu ya fadi [7]). kaddan mutane mahdi sun
soki mutum sun yesda bindiga. mutum kaman ishirin
sun kama. basha ya che ba ẓashi gudu ba har anka-
kamashi. ambugashi da bindiga ankasareshi da takobi.
mahdi ya che akawo kainsa ansareshi andoka namansa
anjefashi chikkin rua. kainsa anakawo wurin mahdi.
mahdi ya che rufe idanu ya che kun yi mugun abu
domi ku kassheshi ya yi fushi ya tashi ya komo sansanni da marechi.

On the day on which the city was going to be
captured the war was carried on from morning till night
without any respite. Many of the Pasha's men and
many of the Mahdi's men were killed, this went on
till evening, till the early dawn. The Pasha's men left
a certain place and came to the place where the Mahdi
was and said, we are tired and have had no rest today,
give us something to eat, if you come to the house
to night the Pasha will run away. The Mahdi said it is

well, we will do so, we will capture him. The Mahdi
gave them goods, he said, go if you wish, or stay in
the camp, if you do not wish to go to your own place.
They rejoiced; he brought them an ox, it was killed,
a camel also was killed (for eating), he brought much
money, he gave it to the soldiers he said, it is well, I
do not wish that he (the Pasha) should sleep before we
capture him, by the power of God.

Then they rose up in the early morning, he brought
his men, they went to the east towards Khartum,
(others) went to the north, the Mahdi himself went
from there towards the south, he rose up and blew a
trumpet, they all went to Khartum. The men of Khartum rose up, they met, they fought one with another
they fired guns, they fought till the evening, they were
not able to enter, the fight went on till break of day
till the early dawn, (then) the Mahdi entered the town.

When the Pasha's men heard this their heart fell.
When the Mahdi's men pierced anyone (with a spear)
they threw away their guns. About twenty men captured the Pasha, he said that he would not run away
till he was captured, he was shot with a gun, he was
cut with a sword. The Mahdi said that his head was
to be brought, it was cut off and taken; his body was
thrown into the water; his head was taken to the place
where the Mahdi was. The Mahdi said, close his eyes,
he said, you have done a wicked thing, why did you
kill him; he was angry, he rose up, he returned to the
camp in the evening.

NOTES.

1) *chimu* 'feed us' chidamu would have been more correct. 2) The use of the Past or Aorist tense in Hausa, where we should expect the Future, is very common. cf. p. 60. 3) *wanan da wanan* 'one and another', for this use cf. p. 20. 4) *bindiga* the singular is here used for the plural. 5) *gari ya wayi* 'the day dawns' lit. the place becomes light, *dunia ya wayi* is used in a similar way. 6) *jijifi* 'the twilight just before the dawn'. cf. Lesson XXII. 7) *zuchiansu ya fadi* lit. 'their heart fell', *zuchia* is here used as masculine.

The above description was dictated by a Hausa pilgrim who passed through the Mahdi's camp on his way to Mecca just after the fall of Khartum.

IV.

Description by a Hausa pilgrim of the ceremonies performed at Mecca.

su zo kusa rua na yemma su yi kamandasu so wuchi kuma har bokkoi. hakka ataffo wurin ka'aba [1]) suna duba daki [2]) samari shina maganasu suna yi kaddan su gumma [3]) su rufe ido su fitto su taffi wurin tsayawa anabi ibrahim su yi ṣalla so biu su tashi duka samari nan shina maganasu suna yi kaddan su gumma su rufe ido su taffi dakin zumzum [4]) su sha su yi wonka su je wojen kofa ṣafá [5]) kaddan su kusa da bakin kofa safá su komo su lashi duchi [6]) su fitta akofa su tsaya bakin kofa su yi magana su sauka suna yi magana su taffi wurin safá su howa bissa su che bismillah allah akbar. su sauka sun je wurin gudu duka sun yi gudu kadan su tsaya su yi taffia su taffi wurin murrowa [7]) su howa bissa murrowa su yi magana su sauka su yi hakkana so bokkoi kana su taffo su yi azki su kawo kurdi maiyawa

abasa samari akawo kuma uba wanzami [8]) saanan su
taffi giddansu su tube zane.

gari ya wayi su taffi mina [9]) su zona ataffi arafa [10])
sun howa bissa tunda hanchi har rana ta fadi. liman [11])
ya che labbe [12]) mutane duka sun che labbe har rana
shi zafi [13]) duka su taffi minna kowa ya doka duchi
bokkoi bokkoi ajefas shetan. akomo duka gidda mutane
masukurdi su sai raguna woni shi sai dari woni dari da
hamsin woni shi sai miatin duka hakkanan ẓasu saya
anyenkasu duka tunda safi hal asai. anazuba achikkin
rami masuchi suna deba anasoiyawa gobi da safi kuma
anyenka kaman jia. mutane su taffii su jefa duchi bokkoi
bokkoi su komo gidda. gobi da safi rana uku su koma
su jefa bokkoi bokkoi sun taffi kuma su jefa nabiu su
koma naüku su jefa su yi aski su kawo riga su sa su
sa wando su sa fulla su yi rawonni anyenka raguna
kaman shekaranjia da asar. ranan fudu mutane duka su
taffi wadansu bissa dawaki wadansu bissa jaki wadansu
bissa alfadari wadansu bissa rakuma saura duka suna
taffia akasa suna taffi wurin da anyenka ismail [14]) su yi
adua su wuchi ẓua mecca askarawa diawa suna buga
madaffa su shiggo mucca su sauka.

They come near to the water on the west, they do
as the others (do), they pass by seven times. Thus they
come to the place of the Kaaba [1]), they behold (its)
house [2]), a young man addresses them; when they have
finished this they close their eyes, they come out, they
go to the place where the prophet Abraham stopped,
they offer prayer twice, they all rise up, the young
man addresses them; when they have finished this they

close their eyes, they go to the house of Zemzem⁴),
they drink, they wash, they go outside the door Safa⁵),
when they come near to the edge of the door Safa,
they come back, they kiss the stone⁶), they go out of
the door, they stop at the threshold of the door, they
utter (certain) words, they sit down, they utter (more)
words, they go to the place of Safa, they mount up
on it, they say, in the name of God, God is great.
They come down, they go to the place of running, they
all run; when they stop they make their journey, they
go to the place of Murrowa⁷), they utter (certain) words,
they sit down. They do this seven times, then they
come, they shave, they bring much money; a present
is given to the young man, a razor⁸) is brought, then
they go to their houses, they take off their clothes.

When the day dawns they go to Mina⁹), they sit
down there, they go to Arafa¹⁰), they mount up on
it, (they stay there) from early morning till sunset. The
Liman¹¹) says 'labbe'¹²) they all say 'labbe' till the
sun¹³) is hot; each takes seven stones, they pelt the
evil spirit, they all return home, those who have money
buy rams, one buys a hundred, another a hundred and
fifty, another two hundred; all will thus buy rams,
they are all killed from morning till late in the afternoon; the flesh is poured out into a hole, those who
eat take out the cooked (food).

On the following morning again (rams) are killed as
on the previous day; the men go, they throw seven
stones each, they return home. On the morning of the
third day they go back, they throw seven stones each,
they go back, they throw them a second time, they

6

go back, they throw them a third time; they shave,
they put on trousers, they put on caps, they make up
their turbans. Rams are killed as on the day before
yesterday in the afternoon.

On the fourth day all the men go away, some on
horses, some on donkeys, some on mules, some on
camels, all the rest go on foot. They go to the place
where Ishmael ¹⁴) was killed, they offer prayer, they
pass on towards Mecca; many soldiers fire off cannon,
they come into Mecca, they sit down there.

NOTES.

1) *kaaba* كعبة for explanatory description of the sites visited by the
pilgrims to Mecca cf. 'Hausaland' pp. 199—203. The Kaaba, which is
believed to have been originally built by Adam, is regarded by the
Mohammedans as the most sacred site in the world.   2) i. e. the sacred
enclosure forming the Kaaba.   3) *gumma* 'to finish' the commoner
form is *gamma*.   4) *zemzem* زمزم the well believed to have been dis-
covered by Hagar.   5) The hill *Safá* صفا, to which the door of the
mosque called by the same name leads, is about fifty paces distant. Before the time of Mohammed it was revered as the abode of the idol
Asaf.   6) i. e. the famous black stone built into the outside of the
Kaaba. It is supposed to have been originally white and to have become black in consequence of the sins of the pilgrims who have kissed
it.   7) *Murrowa* or rather Marwa مروة is another hill not far from
Safá. The ground between the two was that traversed by Hagar in
search for water. The pilgrim is directed to walk seven times over it
with an inquisitive air, now running, now walking, now stopping and
looking anxiously back. It is covered with shops at the present day.
For reference to Safá and Marwah cf. Koran II, 153 'verily S. and M.
are of the institutions of God'.   8) *uba wanzami* lit. 'father of shaving'.
9) *Mina* i. e. Wady Mina the place where Abraham drove the devil
away by pelting him with stones. In imitation of his action the pilgrims throw stones at three pillars erected here.   10) *Arafa* a hill outside Mecca. It is here that the sermon is preached on the first day
of the pilgrimage by a preacher, who is directed to be moved with

feeling and compunction. This is prior to the visit to Wady Mina.
11) *Liman* from Arab. اِمَام *Imam* or priest. 12) *labbe*. This is the
formula of response at the end of the prayers. It comes from the Ar.
لبّى *labi* the II form of which means to pronounce the words لبيك
labbaika 'here I am for your service'. For origin of custom cf. Rel. of
Semites by Robertson Smith p. 411. 13) when *rana* means 'sun' it
is usually masc., when 'day' fem., though the rule is not always ob-
served. 14) according to Mohammedan tradition Abraham attempted to
offer Ishmael, not Isaac, in sacrifice.

V.

Letter addressed to the king of Zinder.

جَغَبَنْ أَيِر يَغِيـدَ سَرِكِنْ زِنْـدِرْ يَغِيسَشِ كُومَ يَغِيسَشِ غَيِسُوَ
دُبُو دُبُو يَثِى اَلْلَهْ يَدَدِى رَنْكَ بَيَنْ حَكَ يَثِى مُو دَوَدَنْدَ
تَارِى دَمُو تُنْدَ كُوَنَ شَفْدُو مُبِرْ كَنُو ۰۰ مُعِنُو كُيِنْزْ دُوَ غَرِنْكَ
مُرْكِيكَ أَبِـرْ مُشِعَ كَسُوَنْ غَرِنْكَ مُبِى ثِنِكِ ثِكِنْ كَسُوَ حَرْ
شَغْلُغْلَمْ سُكَـرِى بَيَنَنْ ذَامْ حَجِ دُوَ مُكَّ ۰۰ مُينْ أَبُـو دُكَ
دَكَفَكَ زَمْنَمْ نَنْ تَاكَ وِتُونُمْ دَغَـنَنْ تَاكَ ۰۰ جَغَبَ يَثِى اِنْ
كَثِى يَكَمَتَ مُتَاشِى نُـو مُتَاشِى اِنْ كَثِر كُيِى شَغْلُغْلَكُ حَرْ
سُكَـرِى نُو مَجِى مُغْدِيكَ دَيَوَ ۰۰ جَغَبَ يَثِى كُومَ كَدَ كَكَرْبَ
دُكَ دَاكْثِى سَبْدَمُ مُودَى فَتَكِ بَا مُو مَاسْفَيْش بَا بَلِى مُسُو
مُثِى كَسَـنْ سَـرِكِ ۰۰ مُرْكِيكَ كُومَ أَبَدَ مُتَنِنْكَ كَدَ سُتَادَمُ
تِيلَسْ سَى مُكَسَمْ غُـزُرِ سَبْدَ تَيِنَنْمْ ۰۰ تَارِى وُتِكَا نَنْ اِنَـا

اَيْكِى غُورُ اَلْمِنِ اَلْلَـهْ شِـبَكَ ثِيْرَ اَلْلَـهْ شِطَوْنْتَ رَنْكَ ۞
اِيَاكَا ۞

V.

jagaban aiyari ya gaida sarikin zinder ya gaisashi
kuma ya gaisashi gaisua dubu dubu ya che allah shi
deddi ranka¹) bayan hakka ya che mu da wadanda
tari da mu tunda kwana sha fudu²) mu ber kano. mu
fito koyanzu zua garinka mu rokeka aber³) mu shigga
kasuan garinka mu yi chiniki chikkin kasua har shegul-
gulamu su kare baya nan zamu haji ẓua mucca⁴). mu
yin abu duka da ka ka fada zamnamu nan taka fitto-
wanmu dagganan taka. jagaba ya che en ka che ya
kamata mu tashi to mu tashi en ka che ku yi shegul-
gulaku har su kare to mu ji mu godeka dayawa jagaba
ya che kuma kadda ka karba⁵) duka da akache saba-
damu mu dai fataki ba mu masufeshe bale⁶) mu so mu
chi⁷) kasan sariki ba. mu rokeka kuma afada mutanenka
kadda su tadamu tilas sai muka samu guzuri sabada
taffianmu. Tari wotiki nan ina aiki goro⁸) alfin. allaḥ
shi baka chira allah shi tsawonta ranka. iyaka⁹).

V.

The guide of the caravan salutes the king of Zinder,
he salutes him again, he salutes him with thousands of
salutations, he says, may God prolong your life; after
this he says, we and those who are with us left Kano
fourteen days ago. We have just come to your town,

we beg of you that we be allowed to enter the market-place of your town, that we may trade in the market until our business is finished: after this we will go forth as pilgrims to Mecca. We will do everything that you tell us, our stay here is in your hands, our going forth hence is in your hands. The guide says, if you say, it is necessary for us to arise, well, we will arise, if you say, do the business that you have until it is finished, well, we will obey, and will thank you much. The guide says again do not believe all the things that are said of us, we are indeed traders we are not brigands, much less do we wish to take the king's country. We beg of you that it may be said to your men that they are not to forcibly disturb us, till we have obtained provision for the way in view of our journey. Together with this letter I send two thousand kola nuts. May God grant you salvation, may God prolong your life! The end.

NOTES.

1) *shi deddi ranka* 'may He lengthen thy life'; one of the commonest forms of salutation addressed to a king. 2) *sha fudu* a shortened form of *goma sha fudu.* 3) *aber* lit. 'it is allowed', cf. p. 27. 4) *mucca.* The town of Mecca is written and pronounced by the Hausas as *mucca.* 5) lit. receive; *ban karba ba* is frequently used for 'I do not believe it'. 6) *bale* 'much more', used with a negative it means 'much less', cf. A. 44. 7) *chi* lit. 'to eat' the regular expression applied to the forcible seizure of a country. 8) *goro* kola nuts form the commonest present given to or by a king; in Zinder the single nut would be worth about two pence. 9) lit. boundary; it forms the usual end to a letter.

VI.

غَـرِنْ شَـمُـوَ

سَرِكِنْ غَر يَنِيِبِى مُتُمْ وُنْدَ يَجِى يَغَ اِنْدَ رَانْ تَكِفُتُوَ يَرْسَ ٠٠
اَنَنْ وَن تَـلَـكَـا مَسِيَيْنِ يَـدُو يَثِى دَسَرِكِ نِتَقِى ٠٠ يَثِى
كَتَقِى ٠٠ اَكِبِى مَس غُزُر يَتَقِى غِـدَ يدَورِى دُوكِنْس سُـرْدِ
يَخَو يَفُتَ دَغَ غَر ذَاشِ اَغُونَنْ اِنْـدَ رَانْ تَكِفُتُوَ يَتَقِى تَـعِىَ
يَسَمْ وَتَ غُـدَ يَـوُثِى ذُكَ يَعِـسَ غَـرِنْ شَمُـوَ ٠٠ دَيَجِى غَـرِنْ
شَمُـوَ اَكِى وَتَ شَمُـوَ تَنَـدُوَ غِدَنْتَ تَكَيِيَ كُوِى ٠٠ دَيَتَقِى غَر
نَنْ شَمُـوَ تَغَنْش ٠٠ اَثِى سُشَمُـوَ نَنْ اَغْرِنْس مُتَـنِى نِى اِنْ
ذَاسُـدُو غَـرِنْـمْ سُكِنْ زَمَى زُنْـرَىَ ٠٠ تَدَوكِيِش تَكَيِيِش غَبَـنْ
سُرِكِ سُكَغِيَس تَكَيِش غِـدَ اَكِبِى مَس كَلِـنِ يَثِى ٠٠ شِكُو بَى
سَنْس بَـا سُكُو سُسَنْش يَتَمْبِيِيس يَثِى كُـدَنْ مُتَـنِى اِنْ
كُكَسَنْنِى سُكَثِى مُنْسَنْگَ يَثِى كَكَ سَنِى سُكَثِى مُنْجِى
غَـرِنْكُ سُكَثِى مَس اِنْ دَمَنَ تَقِى وَن زُنْـرَوَ نِى يَكِلُـوَ عَرِنْكُ
يَثِى شَمُـوَ يَثِى كُنَ شَمُـوَ سُكَثِى مُنَ شَمُـوَ سُكَثِى كَى كُـوَ
اَتَارُ اِن ذَاكَ يَثِى ذَانِى اِنْ غَنُو اِنْـدَ رَانْ تَكِفُتُوَ ٠٠ سُكَثِى
كَدُو كَكَوَنَ دَسَابِ كَـونِى يَـوُنِى دِر يَـبِى جِبِ غَبَـنْ اَرْبَ
كَتَقِى كَعِسْكِى غَر مَيْدُوبُ ٠٠ يَثِى كَـوُثِى يَـوُثِى يَعِس غَر
مَيِجَا يَـوُثِى يَعِـسَ غَر بَرِبِتَ كُوُغِنْ اَزُرْبَا يَدِبِى كَدَنْ يَكْنْس
حَلُنْ رِيغَ يَـوُثِى يَتَقِى رُ مَيِجَا كُوُغِنْ زِنَـرَى يَدِبِى يَدِبِى كَدَنْ

يَكْنْسَ حَنُنْ رِيغَ يَعِسْكِى بَبَنْ غَمْجِ يَوْثِى يَعِسْكِى بَبَنْ

بَور دَدُرْم دَطَمِى تَتَمِى دُوغُوَ .. دَاِت يَطَى بُمْنْدَ بَبَنْ زُنْزَوَ ..

دَاَزْبَ زكَرَ يَثِيرَ رَانَ ذَاتَفْتُو اَكَكُومَ .. جِمَوَ يَثِيرَ حَرْ سَو عُكُو

دَمَيبُدنْ كُوتَا يَذُو يَمُدِى يَثِى رَانَ ذَانَفْتُو يَكُومَ بَدَ رَانَ

ذَاتَفْتُو .. اَتَارْ يَسُكُوَ كِينْ يَذُو غَرِنْ شَمَوَ رَانَ تَكْنِيِش يَذُو

شِدَكِرْ يَسَبْكَ سُكَمِى جِبِيِى يَوْرِكِى .. بُمْنْدَ سَرِكِنْ زُنْزَى

شِيَدَ كُوِى غُدَ دَى تُنْدَ اَكِسِيرِى دُنِيِى يَيِى كُوِى نَنْ يِجَو كَنْسَ

يَكَوْنْثِى بَى كِنْكَسِيِش بَا سَى رَنْدَ دُونِيِى تَكَرِى .. وَنْدَ

يَكَكِيُو حَلِ يَشغَ اِنُوَ تَاسَ وَنْدَ بَى كَكِـمُو حَلِ بَا يَزُونَ اَرَانَ

كُوكِلُوَ تَاسَ تَيِى بُسَ يَغِنِى اِنُونْ بُمْنْدَ يَشغَ بَا .. ..

VI.

garin shamowa.

sarikin gari ya neme mutum wonda ya je ya ga enda
rana ta ki futtowa ya russa. ananan [1]) woni talaka ma-
siachi ya zo ya che da sariki nina taffi. ya che ka taffi.
akayi masa guzuri ya taffi gidda ya dauri dokinsa surdi
ya hau ya futta dagga gari zashi a gunan [2]) enda rana
ta ki futtowa ya taffi taffia ya samu wata guda ya wuche duka ya issa garin shamowa. da ya je garin shamowa. da ya je garin shamowa akoi wota shamowa
tana zua giddanta ta kania [3]) kwoi. da ya taffi gari nan
shamowa ta ganshi. ashe su shamowa nan a garinsu
mutane ni en zasu zo garinmu su kan zama zunzaye.

ta dokeshi ta kaishi gabban sariki suka gaisa ta kaishi
gidda akayi masa kalachi ya chi. shi ko bai sansu ba
su ko su sanshi ya tambayesu ya che ku dan mutane
enna kuka sanni? suka che mun sanka ya che kaka
sanni? suka che mun je garinku suka che masa en da-
muna⁴) ta yi woni zunzua ni ya ki zua garinku? ya che
shamowa ya che kuna shamowa? suka che muna shamowa suka che kai kua ataru enna zaka? ya che zani
en gano enda rana ta ki futtowa. suka che ka zo ka
kwana da safe ka wuni ya wuni derri ya yi jibi gabban
azuba ka taffi ka iske guri maidufu. ya che ka wuchi
ya issa guri maija ya issa guri farifet kwogin ya debe
kaddan azrufa ya kunsa hanun riga⁵) ya wuche ya
taffi wuri maija kwogin zinaria ya debe kaddan ya kunsa hanun riga ya iske baban gamji⁶) ya wuche ya
iske baban baure da darumi⁷) da tsamia⁸) ta taffi dogua.
da ita ya tsaya fufunde⁹) baban zunzua. da azuba zakara
ya china rana zata futto akakuma¹⁰). jimawa ya chira
har so uku da maibudun kofa ya zo ya bude ya che
rana zata futto ya kuma fada rana zata futto. ataru ya
sukua kain ya ƶo garin shamowa rana ta koneshi ya ƶo
shi dakirr ya sabka suka yi jinia¹¹) ya worike. fufunde
sarikin zunzaye shi ya da kwoi guda daia tunda aka-
seri¹²) dunia ya yi kwoi nan ya hau kansa ya kwanche
bai kenkeseshi ba sai randa dunia ta kare. wonda ya
kakiyo¹³) halli ya shigga ennua tasa wonda bai kakiyon
halli ba ya zona arana kokolua tasa ta yi fussa ya gani
ennuan fufunde ba ya shigga ba.

VI.

The country of the ravens.

The king of a (certain) country sought for a man to go and see where the sun comes out and is lost. Presently a poor destitute man came and said to the king, I will go. He said, go. Provision for the journey was prepared for him, he went to his house, he put the saddle on his horse, he mounted, he went forth from the country to go to the place where the sun comes forth. He went on his journey, he spent one month, he passed beyond everything, he came to the country of the ravens. When he came to the country of the ravens, a certain raven was going to its home to lay eggs. When he came to the country, the raven saw him. The ravens indeed in their own country are men. When they are about to come to our country they become like birds. The raven took him and brought him before the king, they saluted; she took him home, dinner was made ready for him, he ate. He, in fact, did not know them; they knew him, he asked them and said, you children of men whence do you obtain your knowledge? They said, we know you; how is it that you know (me)? They said we go to your country; they said to him, when the wet season occurs what bird is it that comes to your country? He said, ravens; he said, are you ravens? They said, we are ravens; they said, you, Ataru, where are you going? He said I come in order to see where the sun comes out. They said, come and stay the night, when the morning

comes, pass the day, when the day is passed and the
night comes, before the dawn of the day after tomorrow go till you arrive at a dark place. He said, pass
on, he came to a red place, he passed on; he came
to a very white place a silver lake, he took a little,
he folded (it) up (in) his sleeve, he passed on, he went
to a red place, a golden lake, he took a little, he
his sleeve he came to a large fig tree, to a durumi
tree, and to a tamarind tree which had grown tall.
On it sat a large bird, the phoenix. In the early dawn
the cock crew, (when) the sun was about to come forth
he (crew) again: after a little he crew a third time,
and the opener of the door came and opened and said,
the sun will come forth, he said again, the sun will
come forth. Ataru galloped in front, he went to the
country of the ravens. The sun burnt him, he came
with difficulty, he lay down, they made (for him) medicine, he was healed. The phoenix is the king of
birds, it has (had) one egg since the world was made,
it laid that egg, it mounted on it, it lies on it, it will
not hatch the egg, till the day on which the world
ends. He who is of a good disposition will come under
its shadow, he who is not of a good disposition will
remain in the sun, his brains will boil, he will see the
shadow of the phoenix, he will not enter it.

NOTES.

1) *ananan* the more usual form is *nan da nan.* 2) *gunan* equivalent
to *wuri nan*, for use of *gun* as a preposition cf A. 25 B. 14. 3) *kania kwoi* 'to lay eggs', the more common expression is *haifi kwoi.*
4) usually written *damana* 'the rainy season'. 5) lit. 'the hand of the

cloak' i. e. its sleeve. 6) *gamji* sometimes written *gimshi*, a large tree affording good shade. 7) *durumi* a large spreading tree under which markets are frequently held in Hausaland. 8) a species of tamarind. 9) sometimes pronounced *huhunde*, probably to be identified with the phoenix. 10) *akakuma* equivalent to *akachira kuma* or it may be a passive form of *koma* to return. 11) *jinia* or *jinya* is a form of sickness, it is here apparently used for a medicine; or we should perhaps translate 'they made a bleeding' i. e. by cupping cf. *jini* 'blood'. 12) *akaseri* apparently equivalent to 'was made'? 13) *kakiyo* an intensive form of *kiyo*.

VOCABULARY.

~~~~~~~~~~

HAUSA — ENGLISH.

Words explained in the notes attached to the readings are not as a rule included in the vocabulary. * after a word means that the word is not used in colloquial Hausa. A. signifies that the word is Arabic and but seldom used in Hausa. Arabic words in frequent use by the Hausas are not specially marked.

a or *aa*, no.

abawa, thick cotton yarn.

abbada or *hal abbada*, for ever.

abduga, cotton, cotton-plant.

abin or *abu* pl. *abubua*, thing.

abin da, the thing which, which.

abinsha, something to drink.

abinchi, something to eat.

abissa, cf. *bissa*.

aboki pl. *abokai*, friend.

abu cf. *abin*.

achike f. *achika* pl. *achiku*, full.

addua, prayer.

agaisheka, hail to you! from *gaishe*, to salute.

ai, really.

aiki, work.

aiki or *yin aiki*, to work.

aiyari, caravan.

aje or *ashe*, really, truly.

ajere, in line.

*akan** if.

akan, above.

akass for *a kasa* on the ground.

akoi, there is, there are.

akunche, untied.

akwia pl. *awaki*, goat. (f.)

ala, A. upon.

alfadari, mule.

alfin, two thousand.

alif, thousand.

alihi, A. his relations.

aljifi pl. *aljifu*, pocket, small bag.

allah, God.

alura pl. *alurai*, needle.

amma, but.

anfani use. *da anfani*, useful.

*anamninche** tale bearing.

araha, cheapness, *da araha*, cheap.

arbaa, four.

arbaïn, forty.

arbamia, four hundred.

ariawa, north.

arziki, good fortune, cf. also D. 3, note.

ashe or *ashi*, cf. *aje*.

ashirin or *ishirin*, twenty.

awanke, washed.

*azaba**, pain.

azrufa or *azurufa*, silver.

azuba, early dawn.

azumi, fast. *yin azumi*, to fast.

ba.....*ba*, not.

ba, to give.

ba, prefix to denote ancestry, cf. p. 56.

baba pl. *mainya*, great.

baba, indigo.

babe f. *babania*, locust.

babu, nothing, without; a contraction of *ba abu* not anything.

bada, to give, cf. p. 58.

ba-haushe, a Hausa native.

bai, a contraction of *ba yi* or *ba ya yi*.

baia cf. *baya*.

baki pl. *bakuna*, mouth.

bakki f. *bakka* pl. *babaku*, black.

bako pl. *baki*, stranger.

bakontaka or *bakonchi*, strangeness. *yi bakontaka*, to feel like a stranger.

ba-laraba pl. *larabawa* an Arab.

bali or *bale*, much more, or (used with negative) much less.

bamda, besides, apart from, in addition to.

banza, in vain, worthless.

bara f. *barania*, hired servant.

barantaka, service.

barao f. *baraunia*, thief.

bashi, to give up, to deliver up to.

bata, to destroy, to spoil, destroyed. cf. p. 58.

batas, *batasda*, to destroy.
batasda hainya to lose
the way.
bature, Arab, white man,
stranger.
bauchi, *bawanchi* or *bauta*,
slavery.
bawa pl. *bayi*, slave.
baya or *baya ga*, behind.
bayes cf. *bashi*.
bayesda, to restore.
ber or *berri*, to leave, to
allow.
berichi or *berchi*, to sleep.
berkono, pepper.
bi, to follow.
biar, *bial*, or *biat*, five.
biggeri, instead of.
bindiga pl. *bindigogi*, gun.
biri pl. *birayi*, monkey.
*birkido**, to come again.
bismi, A. in the name of.
bissa or *bisa*, above.
bissa pl. *bissashi*, beast.
biu or *biyu*, two.
boïya, secret.
bokkoi, seven.
bude or *budi*, to open.
budu, to be open.
budurua, maid.
buga, to strike. *buga buga*,
to strike repeatedly.
bugu bindiga, to shoot.
bunsuru, he-goat.
busa, to blow, trumpet.

chan, there, that, those.
*charkaka**, to sanctify, to
be sanctified.
che, to say.
chi, to eat, to take forcible possession of.
chiawa, grass.
chida, to feed on, to give
to eat.
chika, to fill, full. *chichika*,
to fill quite full.
chikake, full, cf. *achike*.
chikkin or *achikkin* in, into.
dagga chikkin in, from
within.
chiniki, trade, bartering.
yi chiniki, to do business.
chira or *chara*, to crow.
chira or *tsira*, salvation.
chirasda, to deliver.
chishi, to feed on, to give
to eat.
chiwo, sickness. *da chiwo*,
ill, to be ill.

da, to have, to possess.
da, and, with, when, cf.
p. 24.
da . . . . *da*, both . . . . and.
da, free.
da dan, son, native of.
da or *daa*, of old. *lokachin
daa*, in olden time.
dadai, ever, till now; (when
followed by negative statement) never.

dadi, sweet. *ji dadi*, to feel happy. *da dadi*, sweetly.

dafari, at first.

daffa, to cook.

dafafe f. *dafafa* pl. *dafafu*, cooked.

dagga, from.

dagga chan, thence.

dagga enna, whence?

dagganan, hence.

daia, one. *daianku*, one of you. cf. p. 40.

daimu*, for ever.

dainyi pl. *dainyoyi*, fresh, raw.

daki pl. *dakuna*, room.

dakir, with difficulty.

dakka, to beat.

dama, better, cf. p. 45.

damasa*, confusion.

damuna or *damana*, wet season.

dandaka* or *dadaka**, to strike frequently.

dari, hundred.

daria, laughter, *yi daria*, to laugh.

darmi or *darime*, to bind.

dauri cf. *darime*.

dawa, guinea corn, i. e. a small red millet.

dawoiya or *dawoya*, to return to a place at a distance.

dawoiyo or *dawoyo*, to return here.

deddi, to prolong, to increase.

deffi, poison.

derri, late evening, night.

dia, daughter.

diantaka, freedom.

dilali, broker. *yi dilali*, to trade.

dogo f. *dogua* pl. *dogayi*, tall.

doki pl. *dawaki*, horse.

domi, why?

domin, because of.

don, because, because of, in order that.

dorina pl. *dorinai*, hippopotamus.

doro, swelling on the back, hump.

dubu*, to be seen.

dubu, thousand.

duchi pl. *duatsu*, a stone.

duka, all, every.

dukia, goods.

dummi or *dumi*, noise.

dunia, world.

en, whether, that, if, in order that.

enna, where.

errahimi, A. the merciful.

errahmáni, A. the compassionate.

fa, then, therefore.

fada, to fall.

fada or *fadda* or *fadi*, to speak.

fadda or *fada*, to fight.

fandari*, to be crooked.

fansa or *pansa*, reward.

fara pl. *faruna* or *farori*, locust.

farawa, beginning.

fari f. *fara* pl. *farufaru*, white.

faskare, to be unable to do anything. cf. p. 46.

fawa, to slaughter.

fayi, to abound, cf. p. 46.

fet, very, used as a suffix, cf. p. 48.

fi, to excel, to surpass.

fitta or *fita*, to go out from.

fitto or *fito*, to come out from.

fuche cf. *wuche*.

fudu, four.

fufunde, phoenix (?)

fuja cf. *huja*.

fure pl. *furare* or *furayi*, a flower.

fuska pl. *fuskoki*, face.

fussa, to boil.

futa, to rest.

futawa, rest, resting.

futtowa, coming out. cf. *fitto*.

ga, to, for.

ga, to see.

gabba or *gabba ga*, before, in front of.

gabbadai or *gabadai*, together.

gabbaz, east.

gado pl. *gadaji* or *gadoji*, hog.

gado pl. *gadaji*, bed.

gadonia, sow.

gáfera, excuse me! pardon!

gaferta, to forgive.

gaida, to salute.

gaisa cf. *gaida*.

gaisua, salutation, greeting.

gaji, tired.

gajia, weariness. *ji gajia*, to feel tired.

gajiri f. *gajira* or *gajiria*, short.

gamu, to meet with.

ganga pl. *ganguna*, drum.

gara, better. cf. p. 45.

gare or *gari*, to, for. cf. p. 50.

gari pl. *garurua*, place, town, country.

garin, for, on account of.

gaskia, truth. *ba gaskia*, to speak the truth. *da gask*ia, true, truly.

gata, three days hence.

gidda pl. *giddaji* or *giddashi*, house.

girima, great.

giwa pl. *giwayi*, elephant.

gobi, tomorrow, the resurrection day.

godi, to thank.

godia, thanks. *yi godia*, to thank.

godia, mare.
goma, ten.
gona pl. *gonaki*, farm.
goro, kola nut.
gouma, better, cf. p. 45.
guda, times (used with the numerals).
gudu or *guddu*, to run.
gum, with, in the place of.
gun cf. *wuri*.
gurubin or *gun*, instead of.
gusa, to move a little back.
gushe gushe, to gush out abundantly.
guso, to move a little forwards.
guzuri, provisions for a journey.

haifua, birth.
hainya pl. *hainyoyi*, road.
haji, to go on the pilgrimage.
hakika, truly.
hakka or *hakkanan*, thus, likewise.
hakkori, tooth. *hakkorin giwa*, ivory.
halbi, to shoot.
*halita** or *talita**, created being.
halli, disposition.
hamza, five.
hamsin, fifty.
hanchi, two hours after dawn.
hankaka pl. *hankaki*, quail.

hankali, sense, prudence.
da hankali, sensible.
hanu pl. *hanua*, hand.
har or *hal*, until.
hario, again.
hasada, jealousy.
hau, to lift up.
hauia, twenty. cf. p. 38.
hawa, to mount.
hubba, an exclamation expressing astonishment or indignation.
hudu cf. *fudu*.
huja or *fuja*, affair.
huska cf. *fuska*.
hutawa cf. *futawa*.

i or *ii*, yes.
idan, if. cf. p. 52.
ido pl. *idanu*, eye.
iko, power.
iri pl. *irari*, nation, seed, kind.
ishe, to suffice.
iske or *ishe*, to arrive at.
issa, to reach, to be equal to. *da ya issa*, enough.
ita, she. cf. p. 15.
itachi pl. *itatua*, m. a tree, f. a branch cut from a tree.
iya, to be able.
iyaka, boundary, end.
iyawa cf. *iya*.
izan cf. *idan*.

ja pl. *jajayi*, red.

ja, to drag.

jagaba, guide.

jaki pl. *jakuna*, ass.

jaraba*, temptation.

je, to go.

jefa, to throw.

ji, to hear, to obey, to feel.

jia, yesterday.

jibi, the day after tomorrow.

jijifi, the twilight just before the dawn.

jima, to wait.

jimawa, a short time.

jini, blood.

jiuna, one another, cf. p. 23.

ka, thou, thy, cf. p. 15.

kada, spindle.

kadan or *kaddan*, if, when.

kadda, lest.

kaddai or *kadai*, once, only, alone.

kaddan, small, few.

kadi, to spin.

kaffa or *kafa* pl. *kafafu*, foot. *a kaffa*, on foot.

kafo f. *kafa* pl. *kafi*, blind.

kafo pl. *kafoni*, horn.

kai, ho! cf. p. 53.

kai pl. *kanua, kauna* or *kawana*, head; for uses of *da kai*, cf. p. r8.

kai, to carry.

kaia or *kaya*, a load.

kaka or *kakka*, how?

kaka f. *kika*, cf. p. 26.

kalachi, breakfast, dinner.

kalami, A. my words.

kalkadi*, to shake off.

kalkashin, below, under. *dagga kalkashin* from beneath.

kama* f. *kamachi*, fitting.

kama, to seize, to catch.

kaman or *kamal*, like.

(ya) kamata, it is necessary.

kammada or *kamma*, like as, according as.

kana, thou. cf. p. 60.

kane, younger brother.

kanua, younger sister.

kara, reed, reeds.

karami f. *karama* pl. *karamai* or *kanana*, small, little.

karatu or *yi karatu*, to read.

kare, to finish.

karia, falsehood. *yi karia*, to miss fire.

karifi, strength. *da karifi*, powerfully.

karre pl. *karnuka*, dog.

karria, bitch.

kasa pl. *kasashi*, earth, land.

kasshi or *kasshe*, to kill.

kasshi*, to exist.

kasua, market, market place.

kawo, to bring.

kawowa, bringing.

kawichi*, end.

kaza, fowl, chicken.

kaza, such an one. *kaza da kaza*, so and so.

kenkese, to hatch.

kerrin, very, cf. p. 48.

khaliku, A. creator.

khasara or *hasara*, misfortune.

khila*, giving of bribes.

kua, also.

ki, thou, f. cf. p. 15.

kibia pl. *kibo*, arrow.

kifi pl. *kifayi*, fish.

kilago, skin, cow-hide.

kilga or *kirga* or *kedaya*, to count.

kiyo, beauty, goodness. *da kiyo*, beautiful, good.

ko, either, or, even; also used in asking a question.

ko hakka, anyhow.

koda, although.

koenna, anywhere.

kofa or *kwofa*, door.

koiya, to teach, teaching.

koiyo, to learn.

kokolua or *kolua*, skull, brains.

koma, to go back, return.

komi or *komine*, anything, everything. *babu komi* or *ba komi ba*, nothing.

komo, to come back.

konane f. *konana* pl. *konanu*, burnt.

kone, to burn.

kore, to drive away,

kowa, everyone, anyone, any. *babu kowa* or *ba kowa ba*, no one.

kowani or *kowanene* f. *kowachi*, a strengthened form of *kowa*.

koyaushi, at any time, always.

koyanzu, now, immediately.

ku, you, cf. p. 15.

kuda pl. *kudaji* or *kudashi*, fly.

kuddus, south.

kuka, cry, lament.

kuka, you, cf. p. 26.

kulum, always.

kulla, to care for.

kuma, again.

kunche, to loosen.

kurdi or *kudi*, money, price.

kussa or *kusa*, near, nearly, *kussa ga*, near to.

kuturchi or *kuturta*, leprosy.

kuturu, to be leprous.

kwado pl. *kwadodi* or *kwaduna*, toad, frog.

kwana, to sleep, to pass the night. cf. p. 39 note.

kwana pl. *kwanaki*, day.

kwanche, to sleep, to lie down.

kwanta, to spend the night.

kwara, grain, fruit, kernel.

kwarai, rightly, properly.

kwarikwassa, travelling ants.

kwoi, egg, eggs.

lafia, healthy — for use of in salutations cf. pp. 54, 62.

laifi, that which is wrong sin. *bada laifa* (or *laifi*), to condemn.

lasso, twenty, cf. p. 38.

lau, very, cf. p. 48.

litafi, writing, book.

ma, to — for use of cf. p. 50.

ma, verbal prefix. cf. pp. 20, 57.

maaikachi, workman.

machi or *mache* pl. *mata*, woman, female, cf. *mata*.

*machichi**, squeezing.

machiji pl. *machijai*, snake.

mafauchi, butcher.

mai, a prefix — for use of cf. pp. 20, 57.

maibarre, beggar.

maida, to change. *maida himma*, to take care of.

maigidda, owner of house.

maigirima, one who is great.

maigudu, fugitive.

maikaia, carrier.

mairoko, beggar.

maizini, sharp.

makaranta, school.

makafo pl. *makafi*, blind.

mamaki, anything wonderful. *ji mamaki*, to wonder. *yi mamaki*, to make to wonder.

manchi or *manta*, to forget.

maras, without, wanting; used as a prefix.

marechi, evening. *da marechi*, in the evening.

marina pl. *marinai*, dye pit.

masabki, a lodging place.

masaka, weaver.

*masiba**, pain.

massa, quickly.

massa, a small cake.

masufeshe, brigands.

mata, wife, also used as a plural of *machi*.

mi, *mine* or *mineni*, what?

mia, hundred.

miji cf. *namiji*.

mu, we, cf. p. 15.

mugu f. *mugunia* pl. *miagu*, bad, evil.

muka, we, cf. p. 26.

mutane cf. *mutum*.

mutua, death.

mutum or *mutume* pl. *mutane*, man.

na or *-n* of.

-na, my, cf. p. 17.

naam, yes.

nabaia f. *tabaia*, second, that which comes after.

nabiu f. *tabiu*, second.

nade, to roll up.

nadu, to be rolled up, to roll oneself up.

nafari f. *tafari*, first.

*nafsi**, desires.
*nai** for *nasa*, his.
namiji or *miji*, man, male.
nan, here.
nan da nan, immediately.
naüku f. *taüku*, third.
nasa, *nasu*, *nata*, cf. p. 17.
nawa, how much? how many?
nawa, my, p, 17.
nema or *neme*, to search for.
nesa or *da nesa*, far away.
-*nga*, this, cf. p. 19.
ni, I, cf. p. 15.
nia, is it I?
nika, to grind.
-*nka*, -*nki*, thy, cf. p. 17.
-*nmu*, -*nsa*, -*nshi*, -*nsu*, -*nta*, cf. p. 17.
-*nwa*, (inseparable suffix) whose?

rabbi, A. my lord.
rabi or *rabbi*, half.
radda, to whisper, whispering.
rago pl. *ragayi*, an idle person.
rago pl. *raguna*, ram.
rai, life. f. *da rai*, alive.
rakuma pl. *rakumi*, camel.
rana, sun, day, pl. *kwanaki*, days. *rana tsaka*, midday.
randa for *rana da*.

rashin, to be without, without. *rashin karifi*, weak.
rassa, to lose, to be lost.
rataia, to tie, to hang up.
riga pl. *riguna*, tobe, gown, shirt.
rijia, well.
rikichi, deceit.
rimi, silk-cotton tree.
rinni or *rini*, to dye.
rongomi, better, cf. p. 45.
rua pl. *ruaye*, (masc.) water, rain.
rubuï, a quarter.
*rubushi** to lose.
rade, to deceive.
rufi, to close.
russa cf. *rassa*.

sa f. *sania* pl. *shanu*, bull.
-*sa*, his, cf. p. 17.
saa, time, season, hour.
saanan, then.
saanda, when.
saba, to be accustomed.
sabbada or *sabada*, on account of, in exchange for.
sabka or *sapka*, to unload, to alight.
sabo f. *sabua* pl. *sabi*, new.
safe or *safi*, early morning. *da safe*, in the morning.
sahbihi, A. his friends.
sai, quite, only, until, cf. pp. 25, 48, 54.

saida, to buy, cf. *sayi*.

saka, to weave.

sako*, to put down.

salam, A peace.

salla, A to bless.

sallati, A prayer.

sama pl. *sama* or *samania*, heaven.

samu, to find, to take.

sanda pl. *sanduna*, stick.

sania, cow, cf. *sa*.

sanni or *sani*, to know.

sansanchi, to understand well.

sansanni, camp.

sanu, hail! cf. p. 54.

sanu, slowly, gently.

saraunia, queen.

sare, to cut.

sariki or *sarki* pl. *sarikai* or *sarakuna*, king, prince.

sarka pl. *sarka* or *sarkoki*, chain.

sarmayi, a youth.

sarota, kingdom.

sasafi, very early in the morning.

sayes or *sayesda*, to sell.

sayi or *saida*, to buy.

saidina, A. our lord.

sebbaïn, seventy.

settin, sixty.

shamowa, raven, stork.

shanu, cows cf. *sa*.

shashi, half.

shashasha*, to gasp for breath.

sheggeli or *shuggeli* pl. *shugulgula*, business.

shekaranjia, the day before yesterday.

shekkara or *shekara* pl. *shekkaru*, year.

shi, he cf. p. 15. *shi ki nan*, there is, it is so.

shidda, six.

shido*, to take away.

shigga, to enter.

shigasda, to cause to enter.

shika, cf. p. 26.

shiria, preparation, to prepare.

so, to love, to wish.

so, used with numerals thus, *so daia*, once, *so biu*, twice.

soki, to pierce.

su, they, cf. p. 15.

sua, pl. *suaneni*, who, which, what?

suabo, evil. *yi suabo*, to revile.

subuï, a seventh.

sudusi, a sixth.

suka, cf. p. 26.

sukua, to gallop.

subusi, a third.

sumuni, an eight.

suna, name.

surdi pl. *surduna*, saddle.

ta, she, cf. p. 15.

-ta, her, cf. p. 17.

tada, to raise up

taffi, to go. *taffi da*, to take away.

taffia, going, journey.

taffo, to come.

taffowa, coming.

tagua pl. *taguai*, female camel.

taka, thy, cf. p. 17.

takalmi pl. *takalma*, shoe, sandal.

taki f. your, cf. p. 17.

takobi or *takwobi* pl. *takoba* or *takuba*, sword.

taku, your, cf. p. 17.

talauchi, poverty.

talata, *three*.

tallatin, thirty.

tamkar, like as.

tamanin, eighty.

tamu, our, cf. p. 17.

tara, nine.

tara, to collect.

taras or *tarda*, to overtake, to come up with.

tari, to meet, to go to meet, to put together with.

tari, together, *tari da* together with.

taro pl. *tarori*, multitude, abundance.

tarshi, to meet, to help.

taru pl. *taruna*, net.

taru, to assemble.

tasa, his, cf. p. 17.

tata, her, cf. p. 17.

tataka, to tread down.

tausayi, pity, sarrow.

tawa, my, cf. p. 17.

tilas, by force.

tissaïn, ninety.

to, well! so!

tokkos, eight.

toro f. *giwa*, elephant.

tsada or *da tsada*, dear, *expensive*.

tsaga, to tear.

tsatsaga, to tear, to pieces.

tsawo, long, to prolong.

tsaya, to remain, to stand still, to be finished.

tsofo f. *tsofua* pl. *tsofi*, old.

tsofo, an old man. *tsofua*, an old woman.

tsoro, fear. *ji tsoro*, to be afraid.

tsuntsua or *zunzua*, bird.

tsuwa cf. *zua*.

tuba, to repent.

tufa or *tufua* pl. *tufafi* or *tufofi*, shirt, clothes.

tukunia, pitcher.

tumkia pl. *tumaki*, sheep.

tun or *tunda*, as far as, till, since, while as yet.

tunkuda, to push, to butt.

tunyaushi, how long?

turanchi, the Arab language.

uba or *oba* pl. *ubani*, father.

uku, three.

uwa pl. *uwayi*, mother.

wa, A. and.

wa or *wane* m. who, which, what?

wa, elder brother.

wache f. who, which, what?

wai, alas!

wanyi, to end, to finish.

warga for *wogga*, cf. p. 20.

wata, month, *watan yo*, this month, *watan jia*, last month.

wayi, to dawn, *gari ya wayi*, the day dawns.

wochan cf. *wonchan*.

wodanda cf. *wonda*.

wodanga cf. *wonga*.

woddanan or *wodanan* cf. *wonan*.

wofi, empty, bare, worthless.

wogga cf. *wonga*.

woje, outside.

wollata, about 10 am.

wonan pl. *woddanan* or *wodanan*, this near by.

wonchan f. *wochan* pl. *woddanan*, that over there.

wonda f. *woda* or *wodda* pl. *wodanda* or *woddanan*, who, which. *babu wonda*, no one.

wonga f. *wogga* pl. *wodanga*, this near by.

woni who, which?

woni or *wonni* f. *wota* pl. *wonsu*, *wosu* or *wodansu*, some one, some, a certain person or thing.

worga for *wonga*, cf. p. 20.

worigi, play. *yi worigi*, to play.

worike, to heal, to be healed.

wota cf. *woni*.

wotika, letter.

wuche, to pass by.

wur, very, cf. p. 48.

wuri pl. *wurari*, place.

wuri pl. *kurdi*, cowry shell.

wurin, in place of.

wuta, fire.

ya, he, cf. p. 15.

ya, elder sister.

ya, O!

yaka, come!

yaki, war.

yanda, then.

yaushe or *yaushi*, when.

yanzu, now.

yasa pl. *yasosi*, finger.

yarinia, girl.

yaro pl. *yara*, *yarayi* or *yayayi*, boy.

yawo, to go for a walk.

yesda, to throw away.

yi, to do, to make; for idiomatie use cf. p. 52.

yo, to day.

yungwa, hunger. *da yungwa*, hungry.

zaba, to chose.
zaka*, to give tithes, to pray.
zaka, to come.
zaka, a tenth, tithe.
zakara, cock.
zaki pl. *zakoki*, lion.
zakkanin or *tsakanin*, in the midst of.
zakua, coming.
zambar, thousand.
zamna, to rest, sit down, to reside, rest, intermission.
zango, hundred.
zani, I will, I am going.
zani or *zanne* pl. *zanua*, cloth.

zarre, thread.
zikri, A. to utter invocations.
zo, to come.
zona cf. *zamna*.
zua, to, or to comen.
zuba, *zubas*, *zubasda*, to pour out.
zubda, to upset.
zuchia, heart.
zumua, honey.
zungo, halting place for the night.
zunubi* or *zunufi*, sin, evil.
zunzua or *tsuntsua*, pl. *zunzaye*, bird.

ENGLISH — HAUSA.

able, to be *iya*.

above, *bissa, abissa*.

abundance, *tari, dayawa.*
   a. to eat, *zari.*

abuse, *zage.*

accept, to *samu, karba.*

accompany, to *raka, yi rakia.*

accomplish, to *kare, chika.*

accordance, in a. with *kanda.*

according to, *kama, kamada.*

accustomed, to be *saba.*

act, *shinkai*. a. of kindness
   alheri.

advantage, *anfani.*

adversary, *abokin gabba,
   makiyi.*

advice, *dubara, shawora.*

affair, *shuggeli.*

afraid, to be *ji tsoro.*

after, *baya, baya ga.*

afternoon, *azuhur, laasar*
   cf. p. 65.

afterwards, *bavan hakka,
   bayanan.*

again, *kuma, hario.*

agree, to *yi baki daia, yi
   daidai, tangas.*

aid, to *taya, koro sauki,*
   • *yi taimako.*

air, *hiska.*

alas, *wai.*

alight, to *sabka, shido.*

alike, *duka daia, daidai.*

alive, *da rai.*

all, *duka.*

alligator, *kada* pl. *kadodi.*

allow, *beri, ber.*

almost, *kussa.*

alone, *kaddai.*

also, *kua.*

although, *koda, ko.*

always, *kulum, koyaushi.*

amidst, *tsaka, tsakin, zakkanin.*

and, *da.*

anger, *fushi.*

angry, to be *yi fushi, da fushi.*

ankle, *idon kafa.*

annoy, to *wohalshi, haietta.*
anoint, *shafe.*
another, *woni, woni kuma.*
answer, *amsa,* to a. *yi amsa.*
ant, *gara, kwarikwassa, zaggo.*
any, *kowa, kowane.*
anyhow, *kokaka.*
anything, *komi.*
anywhere, *koenna.*
appear, *bayenna.*
approach, *yi kussa.*
Arab, *ba-laraba* pl. *larabawa.* the Arabic language, *turanchi.*
arise, *tashi.*
arouse, *tada.*
arrow, *kibia* pl. *kibo.*
as, *kama, kamada.*
ass, *jaki.*
at, *ga.*
attempt, to *yi kokari.*
await, to *jira.*
awake, to *falka, falaka, falga.*
axe, *gátari.*

back, *baya,* on the b. *reran.*
backwards, *baibai, ringingini.*
bad, *mugu,* pl. *miagu.*
bag, *jika, kankandi.*
ball, *makodi.*
banana, *ayaba.*
bank, *rafi.*

basin, *kasko, akoshi.*
basket, *samfo, gufa, kwando, marari.*
be, to *ni, ki, chi, che* cf. p. 20. to exist, *kasshi.*
bead, *murjan, tasbi, tsakia,*
bean, *wake.*
beast, *bisa, naman daji.*
beat, to *buga, daka.*
beautiful, *da kiyo.*
because, *don, sabada, domi* (eg. *dominsa,* because of him.)
become, to *kawa, zama.*
bed, *gado.*
bees, *kudashen-zumua.*
before, *gabba, gabba ga.*
beg, to *roko,* to b. alms, *yi barra.*
beggar, *maibarra, masarchi, mairoko.*
beget, to *haifi.*
begin, to *fara,* beginning, *farawa.*
behind, *baya, dagga baya.*
believe, to *bada gaskia.*
besides, *bamda.*
better, *mafichi dagga,* cf. p. 45.
between, *tsaka, tsakin.*
bewail, to *yi kuka.*
bind, to *damre, darime.*
bird, *zunzua, tsuntsua.*
birth, *haifua.*
bitch, *karria.*
bite, to *chiso.*

bitter, *doachi*, *tsami*.

black, *bakki*.

blacksmith, *makeri*.

blessing, *alberka*.

blind, *kafo*, b. person *ma-kafo*.

blood, *jini*.

blow, to *busa*.

blue, *shudi*, *shuni*.

blunt, *dallashi*, *taderishi*.

boast, to *takama*.

boat, *jirigi*.

body, *jiki*.

boil, to *fassa*, *tafasa*.

bone, *kasshi* pl. *kasusua*.

book, *kundi*, *litafi*.

boot, *karufa*, *safe*.

borrow, to *ramche*.

bosom, *kirji*.

bottle, *dalulu*, *tulu*, *tukunia*.

boundary, *iyaka*.

bow, *baka*.

box, *sanduki*.

boy, *yaro*, *samri* pl. *samari*.

brains, *kokolua*, *kolua*.

branch, *reshe*, *itachi*, *gain-yen itachi*.

brass, *jan-karifi*.

brave, *da zuchia*.

bread, *gurasa*.

break, to *karie*, *fashi*.

breakfast, *kalachi*.

breath, *lunfashi*.

bridle, *lisami*.

brigands, *masufeshe*, *mafasa*.

bring, to *kawo*.

broad, *fadi*, *maifadi*.

brother, *dan-uwa*. elder b. *wa*. younger b. *kane*.

bruise, to *falfassa*.

brush, to *shafe*.

bucket, *guga*.

build, to *gina*, *kaffa*.

bull, *sa*, *bauna* pl. *bakani*.

burn, to *kone*.

bury, to *bisne*, *bizne*.

bush, *rukoki*, *daji*.

business, *shuggeli*. it is not your business, *babu ru-anka*.

but, *amma*.

butter, *mai*, *main shanu*.

buy, to *sayi*, *saida*.

calabash, *kwaria*, *kwachia*, *kumbu*.

call, to *kirra*, *kirrawo*.

camel, *rakumi*, f. *tagua*.

camp, *zungo*, *sansanni*.

canoe, *jirigi*.

cap, *tagia*, *fuladara*.

capsize, to *jirikichi*.

caravan, *aiyari*.

carcass, *gawa*.

care, to c. for, *kula*, *kulla*.

carelessness, *sakafchi*.

carpet, *kilishi*.

carrier, *maikaia*, *maikawo*.

carry, to *kai*, *kawo*.

cat, *kenwa*, *musa*, *maggi*, *musuru*.

catch, to *kama*.

caterpillar, *kulba*.
cease, to *daina*.
centipede, *shanshani*.
certain, a *woni*.
certainly, *da gaskia*, *ashe*.
chain, *sarka*, *sasari*, *gigar*.
chameleon, *hawoinia*.
change, to *saya*, *sake*.
character, *halli*.
charcoal, *goï*.
charm, *laya*, *hatumi*.
cheap, *araha*, *da araha*.
cheat, to *zamba*, *zambachi*, *yi zalumchi*.
cheating, *rikichi*, *zalumchi*.
cheek, *kumchi*.
chew, to *tona*, *tsukke*.
chicken, *dan chiako*.
chief, *sariki*, *baba*.
choose, to *zaba*.
clay, *yimbu*.
clean, to *gerta*, *yi sarai*.
close, to *rufe*, *sarkafe*.
cloth, *zanne*.
cloud, *lumshi*, *zirnania*, *gilgishi*.
cock, *zakara*.
cold, *dari*, *funturu*.
collect, to *tara*.
colour, *launi*, *iri*.
come, to *zo*, *taffo*, *zua*.
command, to *hakumta*, *hakumchi*.
condemn, to *kada*, *kashe*.
confess, to *huruchi*.
confuse, to *dama*.

conquer, to *ima*, *yi nasara*.
consent, to *yerda*.
consult, to *yi shawora*.
converse, to *yi battu*, *tadi*, *yi magana*.
cook, to *daffa*, *girke*.
cotton, *abduga*, *abawa*.
cough, *tsari*.
count, to *kedaya*, *kilga*.
country, *kasa*.
cow, *sania*.
crawl, to *rarafe*.
crocodile, *kada*.
crow, to *chara*, *kakaruko*.
cruel, *maikelachi*, *maimuni*.
cubit, *kamu*.
cure, to *worike*.
curse, to *zage*.
cuscus, *wassa wassa*.
custom, *ada*, *tada*.
cut, to *yenke*, *sare*.

dark, *dufu*.
dart, *gario*, *hargi*, *hankaltilo*.
date, *dabino*.
daughter, *dia*.
dawn, *azuba*. it dawned, *gari ya wayi*.
day, *rana*, *kwana*.
dead, *matache*, *mutu*.
deaf, *kurma*.
dear, *tsada*, *da tsada*.
death, *mutua*.
debt, *bashi*.
deceit, *wayo*, *mantua*, *munafuchi*.

decrease, to *ragu*, *reggi*, *towaiyo*, *tauwi*.
deep, *zurufi*.
defeat, *artai*.
delay, *daddewa*.
deny, to *musu*, *ki*.
depart, to *rabu*, *fitta*.
desert, *hamada*.
deserter, ie. in war, *kazum*.
deserve, to *chinchinta*.
desire, to *maradi*, *nuffe*.
despise, to *rena*, *ki*.
destroy, to *bata*, *halaka*.
devil, *ebliz*, *shaitan*.
die, to *mutu*.
difference, *dabamchi*.
difficult, *da wuya*.
dig, to *tona*, *gina*, *haka*.
disease, *chiwuta*.
dismount, *sabka*, *shido*.
dispute, *gerdama*, *tsamki*.
distant, *da nesa*.
distribute, to *raba*.
do, to *yi*.
doctor, *maimagani*.
dog, *karre* f. *karria*.
donkey, *jaki*.
door, *kofa* or *kwofa*.
doubt, to *da zuchia biu*, *sauraro*, *yi kokonto*.
dove, *kurichia*.
draw·, to *ja*, *jawo*.
drink, to *sha*.
drive, to *kore*, *iza*.
drop, to *saki*.
drop, a *duggo*.

drought, *farin yungwa*.
drum, *kiddi*, *ganga*.
drunkenness, *hajijia*.
dry, to *shainya*.
dry, *kekashe*.
dry-season, *rani*.
dumb, *kurum*, *bebe*.
dust, *kura*.
dye, to *rinni*.
dye-pit, *marina*.
dysentery, *gudun dawa*.

each, *kowa*, *kowane*.
ear, *kune* pl. *kunua*.
early, *dawuri*. very early, *sasafi*, *da wuriwuri*.
earth, the *dunia*. soil *kasa*.
east, *gabbaz*.
eat, to *chi*.
edge, *kaifi*.
egg, *kwoi*. egg shell, *kambori*, *kwosfofi*.
eight, *tokkos*.
eighteen, *goma sha tokkos*.
eighth, one *sumuni*.
eighty, *tamanin*.
elbow, *diddigan hanu*.
elephant, *toro* f. *giwa*.
eleven, *goma sha daia*.
empty, *wofi*.
end, *makari*.
endeavour, to *yi kokari*.
endure, ie. to last, *karko*, *dauri*. to be patient, *jimri*.
enemy, *abokin gabba*, *makiyi*, *maikinji*.

enough, it is *ya issa, ya koshi.*
enter, *shigga.*
entrust, to *bada, yi sabtu.*
envy, *kita, kiji.*
equal, *daidai.* to make e.,
   daidaita.
escort, *rakia.*
evening, *marechi.*
ever, eg. have you ever
  done so *ka tabba yin hakka.*
every, *kowa, kowane.*
everything, *duka komi.*
evil, *mugu.*
example, *koikoiya.*
except, *sai, saidai.*
exchange, to *sake, yi musaia.*
excuse, to *gáfera.*
exist, to *kasshi.*
experiened, *goni.*
explain, to *waye.*
eye, *ido* pl. *idanu..*

face, *fuska.*
fade, to *fofi, kwake.*
faint, to *suma, yi suma.*
fall, to *fadi, saraya.*
falsehood, *karia.*
family, *dengi, iyali.*
famine, *yungwa.*
fan, *fifiche, faifai.*
far, *nesa.*
farm, *gona.*
fat, *kissi, kibba.*
father, *uba, oba.*
fatigue, *gajia.*
fear, *tsoro* to f. *ji tsoro.*

feast, *buki, idi.*
feed, to *chida, dora.*
feel, to *ji.*
female, *machi.*
fever, *massasara, zazzabi.*
few, *kaddan.*
fifteen, *goma sha biar.*
fifty, *hamsin.*
fig, *baure.*
fight, to *fadda, yi fama.*
fill, to *chika.*
find, to *samu.*
fine, *da kiyo, kallo kallo.*
finger, *yasa.*
finish, to *kare, gama,*
  gumma.
fire, *wuta.*
first, *naferko, nafari.*
fist, *kifi.*
five, *biar, bial.*
flesh, *nama,*
fling, *jefa.*
flower, *fure.*
fly, *kuda* pl. *kudashe.*
follow, to *bi.*
food, *abinchi.* f. for journey,
  guzuri.
foot, *kafa, taki.*
force, *karifi.* by f. *tilas.*
forehead, *goshi.*
forest, *daji.*
forget, to *manchi.*
forty, *arbaïn.*
four, *fudu.*
fourteen, *goma sha fudu.*
fowl, *kaza.*

fox, *karambiki*, *kurege*.
freedom, *diyanchi*.
fresh, *dainye*.
friend, *aboki*.
frighten, *bada tsoro, tsorata*.
from, *dagga*.
fruit, *dia*.
fugitive, *maigudu*.
full, *chika, achika, fau*.

gain, *riba*.
ghost, *fatalua*.
gift, *kiyota*.
girdle, *damarichiki, guru*.
girl, *yarinia*.
give, to *ba, bada, bashi*.
gladness, *murna, farinchiki*.
go, to *taffi, je*.
goat, *akwia*, he goat *bun-suru*.
God, *allah*.
gold, *zinaria*.
good, *nagari* f. *tagari*.
goods, *dukia*.
goose, *dumnia*.
grain, a *kwara*.
grand-father, *haka* f. *hakata*.
grass, *chiawa, haki*.
grave, *kushiya*.
great, *baba, girima*.
green, *algus, chanwa*.
grind, to (eg. corn) *nika, dadaga*.
ground, *kasa*.
grow, to *chiro, chire, yi girima*.

guide, *jagaba*.
guinea-corn, *dawa*.
guinea-fowl, *zabua*.
gun, *bindiga*.

hail, *kankara*.
hair, *gashi*.
half, *shashi, rabbi*.
hand, *hanu*.
hang, *rataya, rataia*.
hard, *tauri*.
hare, *zomo*.
harvest, *kaka*.
haste, *hansari*.
hat, *malafa, gurumfa*.
hatch, to *kenkese, kenkeshe*.
hatchet, *fantaria, gátari*.
hate, to *ki*.
hawk, *shirwa*.
he, *ya, shi*.
head, *kai*.
health, *lafia*.
hear, to *ji*.
heart, *zuchia*.
heat, *zafi*.
heathen, *kafir* pl. *kafirawa, arna*.
heaven, *sama, aljenna*.
hedge-hog, *bushia*.
heel, *duduge, diddiga*.
help, *taya*.
hence, *dagganan*.
her, *-ta, -nta, nata, tata*.
here, *nan, wuri nan*.
hide, to *boiye, rufe*.
hide, *fata, kirigi*.

high, *dogo.*
hill, *tudu, kudunia, tsauni.*
hinder, to *hanna.*
hippopotamus, *dorina.*
hire, to *yi sufuri, sufurchi.*
his, *-sa, -nsa, nasa, tasa.*
hog, *gado.*
hold, to *rike.*
honey, *zumua.*
hornet, *zanzaro.*
horse, *doki* f. *godia.*
hot, *da zafi,* hot water, *ruan demi.*
hour, *saa, lokachi.*
house, *gidda.*
how, *kaka.*
how long, *tunyaushi?*
hundred, *dari, mia.*
hunger, *yungwa.*
husband, *miji.*
hush, to *yi kawoi.*
hyaena, *kura.*

I, *ni, na, ina.*
idle, *rago.* to be idle, *huji.*
idleness, *sausauchi.*
idol, *tsafi, gumki.*
if, *en, kadan, idan.*
ill, *maichiwo, marili.*
illness, *chiwuta.*
imitate, *koikoiya.*
in, *a, ga, dagga-chiki.*
increase, to *dada, dedde, kara.*
indiarubber, *dunko.*
indigo, *baba.*
infant, *jinjere, shariri.*

injure, to *jima, bata.*
ink, *tadowa, tafowa.*
inquire, to *tambaya.*
instead of, *gurubin, biggeri.*
iron, *karifi,* iron ore, *matamachi.*
ivory, *hakkorin giwa, haurin giwa.*

jackal, *dila, kalkechi.*
jaw, *kumatu.*
join, to *gama.*
joint, *gabba* pl. *gabbobi.*
journey; *taffia.*
joy, *murna.*
jump, to *tuma.*

keep, to *rike.*
kick, to *harbi, shure.*
kill, to *kasshe.*
king, *sariki.*
kingdom, *sarota.*
knee, *guiwa.*
kneel, to *durugussa.*
knife, *wuka, konga.*
knot, *kubli.*
know, to *sani, sanni.*
kola-nut, *goro, ibi, atarus.*

lamb, *dan tumkia.*
lame, *gurugu, maigwami.*
lamp, *fitilla.*
land, *kasa.*
large, *baba, babba.*
last, *nabaya.*
late, *makara.*

8

laugh, to *yi daria*.

lawful, *halal*.

lead, *dalma*.

leader of caravan, *jagaba*, *madugu*.

leaf, *gainyan itachi*.

lean, *rame*.

learn, to *koiyo*.

leave, to *ber*, *beri*.

left, *hauni*.

leg, *kafa*, l. irons, *gigar*.

lemon, *lemu*.

lend, to *aro*, *bado aro*.

leper, *maikuturta*, *kuturu*.

leprosy, *kuturta*, *kuturchi*.

lessen, to *rage*.

lest, *kadda*.

letter, *wotika*, *takerda*. l. of alphabet, *harifi*.

lie down, to *kwanche*.

life, *rai*.

lift, to *tada*.

light, *haske*. to l. a fire, *hassa wuta*, *fura wuta*.

light, (not heavy) *sakkai*, *shakup*.

lightning, *wolkia*.

like, *kama*, *tamka*.

lion, *zaki*.

lip, *lebo*, pl. *lebuna*.

listen, to *sorare*.

little, *karami*, *kaddan*, *kankani*, *kalila*.

lizard, *kadangari*, *gusa*.

locust, *fara*, *farandere*, *babe*, *dungo*.

long, *da tsawo*, *dogo*.

looking glass, *madubin fuska*.

loom, *takala*.

loose, to *kunche*, *sunchi*.

lord, *ubangiji*.

lose, to *rassa*, *tabi*, *bache*.

loss, *birna*, *taaddi*, *asara*.

love, to *so*.

lowing of oxen, *boda*.

lungs, *kufu*, *fufu*.

mad, *maihauka*.

make, to *yi*.

male, *namiji*, *miji*.

man, *mutum*.

many, *tari*, *yawa*, *dayawa*.

mare, *godia*.

marks, tribal, *shaushawa*, *keskestu*.

mat, *arsaberi*, *amame*, *taberma*, *keso*.

meaning, *guzu*, *manaa*, *tushi*.

meat, dried, *kilishi*.

meet, to *iska*, *gama da*.

melon, *dila*.

melt, to *narike*.

mend, to *gerta*.

messenger, *jekada*, *manzo*.

midday, *rana tsaka*.

milk, *nono*.

miss, to *kuskure*, t. m. fire, *yi karia*.

misunderstand, to *gigishi*.

mix, to *dama*, *gangama*, *forauforau*.

money, *kurdi*.

monkey, *biri*.
month, *wata*.
moon, *wata*.
morning, *safi*, *safia*, *hanchi*.
mosquito, *sauro*, *sabro*.
mother, *uwa*.
mount, to *hawa*.
mouse, *bira*, *dambaria*.
move, to *mosa*, *yi mosi*.
much, *dayawa*, *yawa*, *ma-yawa*.
mud, *laka*, *tabo*.
my, *-na*, f. *-ta*, *nawa*, f. *tawa*.

naked, *funtu*.
nakedness, *chirara*.
name, *suna*.
narrow, *kunche*.
near, *kussa*.
neck, *wuya*.
needle, *alura*.
neighbour, *makofchi*.
net, *taru*, *koma*, *raga*.
never, *dadai* (when combined with negative particle).
new, *sabo*.
news, *labári*.
night, *derri*.
nine, *tara*.
nineteen, *goma sha tara*.
ninety, *tissaïn*.
no, *aa*.
noise, *dummi*.
none, *ba kowa*, *babu wonda*.
north, *ariawa*.
nose, *hanchi*.

not, *ba ... ba*.
nothing, *babu*, *babu komi*, *ba komi ba*.
now, *yanzu*, *koyanzu*.
nut, *gujia*, *gedda*.

obey, to *ji*, *bi*.
obtain, to *samu*.
officer, *dogari*, *zarumi*.
old, *tsofo*, to grow old, *tsufa*.
once, *so daia*.
one, *daia*.
onion, *albasa*.
only, *kaddai*.
open, to *bude*, *fuda*, *balla*.
or, *ko*.
ordeal, *gwaska*.
ostrich, *jimina*.
other, *woni*. others *wodansu*.
our, *-mu*, *namu*, f. *tamu*.
outside, *woje*, *dagga woje*.
oven, *tanda*.
over, *bissa*, *abissa*.
overtake, to *tarshi*.
owe, to — he owes me, *shina da bashina*.
owl, *mushiye*.
ox, *sa*, *takarikari*.

pain, *saggi*, *zogi*.
palm, of hand, *tafin hanu*.
palm tree, *tukurua*, *giginia*.
palm-wine, *bam*.
paper, *takerda*.
pardon, to *gáfera*, *yafe*.

parrot, *aku.*
part, *rabbi.*
pass, to *wuche, shudi.*
path, *turuba, hainya.*
patience, *hankuri.*
pawpaw, *gonda.*
peel, to *kankari, bare.*
pen, *alkalami.*
pepper, *berkono,* *tushi,* *tamka, masoro, kimba.*
perhaps, *wotakila.*
perish, to *bachi, mutu.*
perspiration, *zufa.*
pierce, to *soke.*
pig, *gado.*
pigeon, *tandabara.*
pilgrim, *haji.*
pipe, *tukunian taba.*
pit, *rami.*
pity, *tausayi.*
place, *wuri,* to p. *sa.*
plain, *fakko, fili.*
plank, *gungumi.*
plant, to *yi shipka.*
play, *worigi.*
please, to *gumshe,* it pleases me, *ya gumsheni.*
pluck, to *chire, chiro, chirasda.*
poison, *deffi.*
pond, *kurduduffi.*
pony, *kuru, doki kuru.*
poor, *talaka.*
pot, *tukunia, kasko.*
pour, to *zubo, zuba.*
power, *iko, karifi.*

praise, *yabo, yabbo.*
pray, to *yi salla, yi adua.*
prefer, to *fisso, fi.*
preparation, *shiri.*
present, a *abin gaisuwa, kiyota.*
press, to *taushe.*
pretend, to *ria, maida kansa.*
prevent, to *hanna, tankwasa, tare.*
price, *kurdi.* its price, *hakinsa, tamaninsa.*
pride, *fadinrai, fadinzuchia.*
promise, to *yi magana daia, yin alkaweli.*
proof, *shaida.*
prophet, *anabi.*
pull, to *ja.*
pumpkin, *kabiwa, goji.*
punish, to *palashi.*
push, to *tunkuda.*
put, to *sa, aje.*

quarter, *rubui.*
quarrel, *fusuma, gerdama.*
queen, *saraunia.*
question, to *tambaya.*
quickly, *da sauri, massa massa, mazza mazza.*
quiet, to *yi shiru, yi kurum.*
quiver, *kwori.*

rabbit, *zomo.*
rag, *tsuma* pl. *tsumoki.*
rain, *malka, maku, sarafa.*

rainy-season, *damana*, *ba-sara*.
raise, to *tada*.
ram, *rago*.
rat, *jaba*, *kusu*.
raven, *shamowa*.
read, to *yi karatu*.
ready, *shiri*.
reap, to *girbi*.
receive, to *samu*, *karba*.
red, *ja*.
reed, *kara*.
refuse, to *ki*.
rejoice, *yi murna*.
relation, *dengi*, *kotana*.
remainder, *saura*, *kingi*.
remember, to *tuna da*.
remove, to *kauda*, *kawas*.
repent, to *tuba*.
rest, to *futa*, *futawa*.
return hither, to *komo*, *da-woiyo*.
return thither, to *koma*, *da-woiya*.
revenge, *rama*.
rice, *shinkafa*.
rich, person, *maidukia*.
ride, to *hawa doki*, *kilisa*.
right-hand, *dama*.
ring, *zobe*.
ripe, *nena*.
rise, to *tashi*.
river, *koramma*.
rob, to *sache*, *yi sata*.
room, *daki*.
root, *saiwa*, *guzun itachi*.

rope, *igia*.
round, *kumbu*, *shankumbu*.
run, to *gudu*.

sack, *jika*, *taiki*, *buhu*.
sacrifice, *sadaka*.
saddle, *surdi*.
salt, *gishiri*.
salute, to *gaida*, *gaishe*.
salutation, *gaisua*.
sand, *rairai*.
sandals, *sambazai*.
satisfied, to be *koshi*.
save, to *cheche*, *cheto*.
saw, *sasago*.
say, to *che*, *fada*.
scatter, to *walwache*, *kari-riye*.
school, *makaranta*.
scorpion, *kunami*.
seat, *kujira*, *kushira*.
second, *nabiu* f. *tabiu*.
secretly, *boya*, *da boya*.
seed, *iri*.
seek, to *nema*, *bida*.
sell, to *sayes*, *sayesda*, *talla*.
send, to *aiko*, *aiki*.
separate, to *raba*.
servant, *bara*.
seven, *bokkoi*.
seventeen, *goma sha bokkoi*.
seventy, *sebbain*.
sew, to *dumke*.
shade, *enuua*, *enua*.
shame, *kumia*.
sharp, *da kaifi*.

shave, to *aske*.

she, *ta*, *ita*.

sheep, *tumkia*.

shield, *gerkwa*, *kutafani*.

shirt, *tugua*.

shoot, to *halbi, buga bindiga*.

short, *gajiri*.

show, to *nuna*, *goda*.

shut, to *rufe*.

side, *sassa, woje*. s. of body, *kwibi*.

silk, *alharini*.

silk-cotton-tree, *rimi*.

silver, *azurufa*.

sin, *zunufi*, *laifi*.

sing, to *yi waka*.

sister, elder, *ya*. younger, *kanua*.

sit, to *zamna*.

six, *shidda*.

sixteen, *goma sha shidda*.

sixty, *settin*.

skill, *dubara*, *goni*.

skin, *fata*, *kirigi*.

sky, *sama*, *samma*.

slave, *bawa* pl. *bayi*.

slavery, *bauchi*, *bauta*, *bawanchi*.

sleep, to *yi berichi, yi berchi*.

slip, to *kubche*.

slowly, *sanu sanu*.

small, *kanane*, *kankanta*.

small-pox, *agana*.

smell, to yield a bad *yi doi*. to yield a good s. *bada kamshi*.

smoke, *hayaki*.

snail, *tantanua*.

snake, *machiji*.

snuff, *garintaba*, *tabanhanchi*.

so, *hakka*, *hakkanan*.

soap, *sabuni*, *sabunin sello*.

soft, *tafshi*, *tafshi tafshi*.

soldier, *askar* pl. *askarawa*, *dan yaki*, *saati*.

some, *woni . . . woni*, *wosu*, *woddansu*.

sometimes, *woni yayi*.

son, *da*.

soul, *kurua*.

south, *kuddus*, *kudu*.

sow, to *yi shipka*.

sparrow, *baiwan-allah*.

speak, to *yi magána, fada*.

spear, *mashi*, *maji*, *haggu*, *hankaltilo*.

spider, *gizzo*.

spin, to *kadi*, *yi zarre*.

spoon, *chokali*.

spread, *shimfida*.

squirrel, *kusum-bissa*.

stand, to *tsaya*.

star, *tamraro*, *tauraro*.

steal, to *sache*, *yi sata*.

stick, *sanda*, *jagora*.

stomach, *tumbi*.

stone, *duchi* or *dushi* pl. *duatsu*.

stork, *maijika*.

story, *tasunia*, *fira*, *aljima*.

straight, *sosai*.

stranger, *bako*, *hadaka*.
strike, to *buga*, *yi mari*.
stumble, to *karro*, *tuntube*.
sugar-cane, *tankanda*.
sun, *rana*.
sun-rise, *gari ya wayi*.
sun-set, *faduan rana*.
surpass, to *fi*, *faye*.
swallow, *tsatsiwa*.
swear, to *ranche*, *yi ran-tsua*.
sweep, to *share*.
sweet, *da zaki*, *da dadi*.
sword, *takobi*, *tagomas*.

take, to *doka*, *dauka*, *karba*, *debe*.
tall, *dogo*.
taste, to *dandana*.
tax, *fito*, *kurdinkasa*.
teach, to *koiya*, *sanasda*.
tell, to *fada*, *fadda*.
ten, *goma*.
tent, *lema*.
thank, to *gode*.
that, *chan*, *wonan*.
theft, *sata*.
then, *saanan*, *yaennan*.
thence, *dagga chan*.
there, *chan*, *wuri chan*.
therefore, *don wonan*, *domi*, *domin hakka*.
thief, *barao*, *maisani*, *mai-sata*.
thing, *abin*, *abu* pl. *abu*, or *abubua*.

think, to *tamaha*, *zetto*, *zachi*.
thirst, *kishirua*.
thirty, *tallatin*.
this, *-nga*, *wonga*, *nan*, *wonan*.
thorn, *kaya*.
thou, *ka* f. *ki*.
thousand, *dubu*, *zambar*, *alif*.
thread, *zarre*, *abawa*, *ar-rafia*.
throw, to *jefa*, *yesda*.
thunder, *aradu*.
thus, *hakka*, *hakkanan*.
time, *lokachi*, *lottu*.
to, *ga*, *gare*, *zua*.
toad, *kwado*.
tobacco, *taba*.
tobe, *riga*, *girika*, *tugua*.
together, *tari*, *gabbadin*.
tomatoe, *gauta*.
to-morrow, *gobi*.
too, *kua*, *ko*.
tooth, *hakori*, *hauri*.
touch, to *tabba*.
town, *birni*, *gari*.
trader, *fatake*, *maichiniki*, *dan kasua*.
tree, *itachi*, *itche*.
trouble, *wohalla*.
true, *da gaskia*.
truly, *aje*, *ashe*.
try, to *yi kokari*.
turkey, *talatalu*.
turn, to *juya*.

twelve, *goma sha biu.*
twenty, *asherin, ishirin, hauïa, lasso.*
twice, *so biu.*
two, *biu.*

understand, to *ji, fahumta.*
unless, *sai, saidai.*
until, *har, hal.*
upset, to *jirikichi.*
us, *mu.*
use, to *aiki da.*
use, *anfani.*

victory, *nassara.*
village, *ungua, gimi.*
vulture, *angulu, augulu, mikia.*

wages, *lada, karo.*
wait, to *jira.*
walk, to *yawo,* to w. fast, *gagawa.*
want, to be in w. of *kasa, rashi.*
war, *yaki.*
wash, to *wanke.*
wasp, *rina, zurnako.*
waste, *birna, banna.*
water, *rua.*
weigh, to *auna, awuni.*
well, *rijia.*
well, it is well! *to.*

west, *yamma.*
wet, to be *jiki.*
what? *mi, mine, mineni.*
wheel, *rumbua.*
when, *yaushi, woni lokachi.*
whence, *dagga enna.*
where, *enna, enda.*
which, *wonda, da, abinda.*
while, *tunda, tun.*
whisper, *radda.*
white, *fari, farifet.*
who? *wa, waneni, wonni.*
who, *wonda, da.*
why, *domi, maiessa,*
wide, *fadi.*
wife, *mata.*
wind, *hiska, iska.*
wish, to *so.*
with, *da, tari da.*
without, *babu, bamda, maras,* to be w. *tabi.*
woman, *machi.*
wonder, to *ji mamaki.*
wood, *itachi, itse.*
wool, *mulufu, sufi.*
word, *magana.*
work, *aiki.*
world, *dunia.*
worm, *tana, tsutsa.*
worthy, *chinchinta.*
wound, *raüni.*
write, to *rubutu.*
wrong, *laifi.*

yam, *doiya*.

year, *shekkara*, last y. *bara*, next y. *baddi*, this y. *banna*.

yellow, *rawaiya*.

yes, *i, hakkana, shi ki nan*.

yesterday, *jia*. the day before y., *shekaranjia*.

you, *ku*.

youth, *sarmayi*.

zealous, to be *da himma*.

NOTE.

———

The pronunciation of the terminal vowel in many of the words given in the above vocabulary, which end in *i* or *e*, is by no means uniform. Thus one native will say *ya wuchi* 'he passed', another in the same district will say *ya wuche*. I have tried to represent the sounds most commonly heard in Kano, but in very many instances (as e. g. in the substantive verb *ni*, *ki*, *chi* or *ne*, *ke*, *che*), it is impossible to say which is the more correct pronunciation.

A similar difficulty exists in regard to many words in which a double consonant occurs. Thus one native will pronounce the Hausa equivalent for 'near' *kussa*, whilst another will say *kusa*. Hausa writing affords no help towards a solution of the difficulty as the mark of reduplication is very seldom inserted even in words where a double consonant is most clearly heard e. g. *massa* 'quickly', *rassa* 'to lose'. In some cases it would seem as though the doubling of the consonant was dependent on the context in which the word occurred. Thus a native would say *fadda mani* 'say to me', but would usually say *ya fada* 'he said'. There are several

words in which the insertion or otherwise of the consonant *y* is not uniform; thus some natives would say
rataia kaia, others *rataya kaya* 'to tie a load'. The
sounds represented by *z* and *ts* are often confused;
thus we have *zunzua* and *tsuntsua* 'bird'; the latter is
the sound as usually written.

The beginner is cautioned against regarding the Hausa
words which are given as equivalents for the various
English expressions as synonyms. In the limits of a
short vocabulary it is impossible to explain minute
differences of meaning, a discussion of which must be
reserved for a dictionary, which is in course of preparation. For a similar reason I have not thought it
necessary to distinguish in the vocabulary between the
letters *z*, *s*, *k*, *h*, *l*, and these letters with a dot below
(cf. p. 12) as the addition of the dot does not represent any variation in the pronunciation.

For EU product safety concerns, contact us at Calle de José Abascal, 56–1°,
28003 Madrid, Spain or eugpsr@cambridge.org.

www.ingramcontent.com/pod-product-compliance
Ingram Content Group UK Ltd.
Pitfield, Milton Keynes, MK11 3LW, UK
UKHW012339130625
459647UK00009B/384